Contents

Boys' Life and Other Plays

BOYS' LIFE

and Other Plays

by

HOWARD KORDER

Grove Press
New York

Printed in the United States of America

Library of Congress Cataloging-in-Publication Data

Korder, Howard.
    Boys' life and other plays / by Howard Korder.
        p.   cm.
        Contents: Boys' life—Fun—Nobody—The middle kingdom—Lip service.
        ISBN 0-8021-3170-0
        I. Title.   II. Title: Boys' life.
PS3561.06567B69   1989
812'.54—dc19   89-1671

Grove Press
841 Broadway
New York, NY 10003

98 99 00 01 10 9 8 7 6 5 4 3

BOYS' LIFE

A Comedy

For Lois

Boys' Life was presented by Lincoln Center Theater (Gregory Mosher, director; Bernard Gersten, executive producer) at the Mitzi E. Newhouse Theater in New York City, opening on February 29, 1988. The Atlantic Theater Company was directed by W. H. Macy; the sets were by James Wolk; the costumes were by Donna Zakowska; the lighting was by Steve Lawnick; the sound was by Aural Fixation; the original music was composed by David Yazbek. The cast, in order of appearance, was as follows:

DON	Jordan Lage
PHIL	Steven Goldstein
JACK	Clark Gregg
KAREN	Mary McCann
MAN	Todd Weeks
MAGGIE	Felicity Huffman
LISA	Melissa Bruder
GIRL	Robin Spielberg
CARLA	Théo Cohan

CHARACTERS

JACK
DON
PHIL

A MAN

LISA
MAGGIE
KAREN
GIRL
CARLA

All in their late twenties

TIME

The present. Various intervals over the course of a year.

PLACE

A large city.

Scene 1

Don's bedroom. JACK *smoking a joint.* PHIL *lying on the floor, wearing a set of headphones.* DON *sitting in his underwear. Bottles, clothes, books scattered on the floor. One* A.M.

JACK: Remember the nineteen-seventies?

DON: Sure. Sort of.

JACK: Name three things that happened in the nineteen-seventies.

DON: This is like a trick question, right?

JACK: I'll give you one minute.

PHIL (*loudly, tapping phones*): I haven't heard this since *col*lege, you know?

JACK (*smiling and nodding*): Eat me, Phil.

PHIL (*not hearing*): Okay!

JACK: Give up?

DON: That wasn't a minute.

JACK: Let's go.

PHIL: *Great* bass line.

DON: Um . . .

JACK: Do it!

DON: Um . . . Watergate? And . . . uh . . . (*Pause.*) The Sex Pistols . . . and . . . uh . . . (*Pause.*) Did I say Watergate?

JACK: I rest my case.

DON: Ah . . . giant leap for a man?

JACK: Oh, hang it *up,* Don.

DON: Did I *say* Watergate?

JACK: You're losing it, Don. Your mind is going.

DON: The nineteen-seventies.

JACK: You're rotting on the vine.

PHIL (*imitating an electric guitar*): War-raaang!

(*Pause.*)

JACK: Well, *I'm* having fun.

DON: Me too.

JACK: I know you are. We live in thrilling days, Don.

DON: We *do.*

JACK: And I think that's swell.

DON: I do too.

JACK: I know you do. You're an agreeable guy. And I've been meaning to tell you this, really, if someone came up to me and asked, "Now this *Don* fellow, what's he all about?" I'd have to tell him, well, darn it, Don, Don's an *agreeable* guy.

DON: I'd go along with that.

JACK: Would you go along with a toast?

DON (*picking up a beer*): By all means.

JACK: To you, Don, for being the postmodern kind of nut you are.

DON: Thanks, Jack.

JACK: To Phil, a great guy in spite of some desperate handicaps.

PHIL (*not hearing*): Okay!

JACK: And to me, for being perfect.

DON: Not easy.

JACK: And Don, to our times together. From campus cut-ups to wasted potentials.

DON: It feels like years.

JACK: It *has* been years.

DON: We are getting old.

JACK: To our parents, Don. To the dream they called America. To the Big Kidder upstairs. To, ah . . .

PHIL (*imitating drums*): Da-dum-dum-dum-dum-*dum* . . .

DON: The ladies!

JACK: Don, a toast, a very *special* toast, to the ladies.

DON: Oh my.

JACK: Yes indeed. Where would we be without them?

DON: We'd be nowhere.

JACK: We wouldn't be *here*.

DON: We wouldn't even *exist*.

JACK: We would not.

DON: It's a sobering thought.

JACK: It's food for thought.

DON: It's a thought to think.

(*Pause.*)

JACK: Well, no sense blaming them for it now.

DON: It's a dead issue.

JACK: It's all said and done. 'Cause when you come right down to it . . .

PHIL: I *love* this part . . .

JACK: A man . . .

DON: Is a *man.*

JACK: He *is* a man.

DON: By *any* other name.

JACK: He'd still smell.

DON: Amen.

JACK: God*damn.*

DON: Goddamn *shit.*

JACK: *Cocksucking* shit.

DON: Goddamn shiteating asshole *scumbags!*

(JACK *breaks out into a wolf howl.* DON *joins in. Pause.*)

You know, you'd never have this kind of talk with a woman.

JACK: No, you wouldn't. And I want you always to remember this, Don. When you're old and pissing in your daybed, remember who brought you out of the jungle and shaved off your fur.

DON (*in a zombie-like monotone*): It was you, master. You teach Don to walk like man.

JACK: And you *better* be grateful. (*He drags on the joint.*) Here. Finish that off. Come on, come on.

(*He passes the joint to* DON. DON *takes a hit. Silence.*)

What are you smiling about?

DON: Nah, I was just thinking.

JACK: Uh-huh.

DON: I used to really want to be an astronaut, you know? Be up there. The quiet. Walter Cronkite talking about me to millions of people. But I wouldn't have to *listen.*

JACK: So?

DON: So I'd still like to be an astronaut.

JACK: Maybe you will be, Don. But even if you were . . . you'd still have to get out of bed in the morning.

DON (*thinking it over*): Yeah.

(*Pause.* PHIL *takes off the headphones.*)

PHIL: Emerson, Lake, and Palmer, man, whatever happened to them?

JACK: They all died horribly, Phil, in a bus crash.

PHIL: They did? That's really depressing.

JACK: I thought it might be. (*Pause.*) Well, gentlemen. Anybody have a good fuck lately?

PHIL: Does masturbation count?

(*Blackout.*)

Scene 2

A child's bedroom. PHIL *and* KAREN *standing at opposite ends of the room, facing each other. The bed is piled with coats. Sounds of a party filter in from outside.*

PHIL: Well, there *you* are.

KAREN: Yes.

PHIL: And here I am.

KAREN: Yes.

PHIL: So here we are, both of us. Together.

KAREN: Talking.

PHIL: Right here in the same room.

KAREN: It's pretty amazing. (*Pause.*) Enjoying the party?

PHIL: Oh, yes. Certainly. Yes yes yes.

KAREN: Mmmm.

PHIL: No.

KAREN: Oh.

PHIL: Not in the larger sense.

KAREN: Why did you come?

PHIL: I was invited. I mean . . . Jack invited me.

KAREN: And you do everything Jack says.

PHIL: No, I . . . he's my friend. My oldest friend. (*Pause.*)
You look great tonight, Karen.

KAREN: Thanks.

PHIL: No, I mean it. Just wonderful.

(*Pause.*)

KAREN: You look good.

PHIL: No.

KAREN: You do.

PHIL: No I don't.

KAREN: Really, you do.

PHIL: Do I?

KAREN: What do you want, Phil?

PHIL: Well, I don't *want* anything. I just wanted to . . . say hello.

KAREN: Hello.

PHIL: Yes, well. (*Pause.*) That's lovely, what you have on, what is it?

KAREN: A dress.

PHIL: I've always admired your sense of humor, Karen.

KAREN: What do you want, Phil?

(*The door opens and a* MAN *pops his head in.*)

MAN: Oh. I'm sorry.

KAREN: We're almost done.

MAN: Oh. Well. Fine. I'll, ah . . . fine. (*He exits, closing the door.*)

PHIL: What was that all about?

KAREN: What?

PHIL: That. That guy.

KAREN: I don't know.

PHIL: Well, you seemed pretty familiar with him.

KAREN: Are you feeling okay?

PHIL: Hmmm? Oh, sure. Things are going really really great for me right now. Just fine. I have my own partition now, over at the office, they put up one of those, ah . . . so *that's* really good. And I'm going to the spa a lot, I'm working ou—well, I can't use the machines 'cause you know of my back, but I love the Jacuzzi, so, actually, it's strange, 'cause I fell asleep in

it, in the whirlpool, and when I woke up I had this
incredible headache, I mean it would *not* go away, I
felt this thing here like the size of a peach pit, I went
for a *blood* test, I was convinced I, you hear all this
stuff now, the way it's spreading, I mean I'm not—
but I was sure I had it.

KAREN: Had what?

PHIL: It. You know.

(*Pause.*)

KAREN: And?

PHIL: I didn't. So.

(*Pause.* KAREN *looks at the door.*)

Anyway, it's funny we both happened to turn up here
tonight, isn't it, 'cause I was just thinking, I was wondering . . . I mean, it's a couple of months since I last
spoke to you and I was just *wondering* if we were still,
you know, seeing each other.

KAREN: *Seeing* each other.

PHIL: Yes.

KAREN: No.

(*Pause.*)

PHIL: All right.

KAREN: We were never seeing each other, Phil.

PHIL: Well, no, not actually *seeing* . . .

KAREN: We slept together once.

PHIL: Twice.

KAREN: You left before I woke up.

PHIL: Okay, yeah, but . . . I mean, *everybody* does that.

KAREN: And you never called.

PHIL: Now . . . now about *that,* you see, I was involved in a very bad kind of situation then, and I wasn't really in a position to, ah . . . as much as I *wanted* to . . . and I *did,* very, very—

KAREN: What do you want?

PHIL (*pause*): Well, I'd like another shot at it.

KAREN: At what?

PHIL: At you. To get to know you.

KAREN: I'm really not worth the effort, Phil.

PHIL: You're seeing someone else, right?

KAREN: That's got nothing to—

PHIL: You *are* seeing someone.

KAREN: Not actually *seeing* . . .

PHIL: No, no, it's fine. Early bird and all that stuff. I'm fine. Everything is fine.

KAREN: It's got nothing to do with you, Phil. There's just a lot of things I have to work through right now. But I like you, I do. You're . . . you're a wonderful person.

PHIL: You're a wonderful person too, Karen.

KAREN: Well, so are you, Phil.

PHIL: That's right. We both are. (*He hugs* KAREN.) Listen to this. A guy in my office has a cabin upstate. He never uses it. It's on the edge of a beautiful freshwater lake. Why don't we go there, just the two of us, we spend the weekend, relax, get out of the city . . . do some straight thinking. What do you say?

KAREN: No.

PHIL: Is it because of this guy you're seeing?

Karen: Well, I'm not actually *seeing*—

PHIL: Then what is it?

KAREN: It's just not a good idea.

PHIL: It's not?

KAREN: No. Not at all. (*Pause.*) You're touching my breasts, Phil.

(*The* MAN *pops his head through the door.*)

MAN: Oh gosh. Beg pardon. (*He shuts the door.*)

PHIL: I think about you a lot, Karen.

KAREN: You do.

PHIL: Yes. At work, you know, the laundromat, in the shower . . . places like that. (*Pause.*) I mean that in the positive sense.

KAREN: I'm not worth the trouble.

PHIL: It's just two days out of your life, Karen. This could turn out to be something really special, it'll be over before you know it.

KAREN: You're making this very difficult.

PHIL: I'm making it incredibly *easy.* Come up to the country with me.

KAREN: Phil—

PHIL: Come.

KAREN: Please, Phil—

PHIL: I'm asking for a *chance.*

KAREN: Oh, no. Oh no. This is coming at a very bad time for me. I don't think I can handle this right now. My life is a real big mess, okay, and . . . I read that by the time you're five you've already developed the major patterns for the rest of your life. I mean whether you're going to be basically happy or . . . a fireman, a lesbian, whatever. And of course it's not fair at all, because nobody tells a little kid anything about that. But that's the way it is. So I've been thinking about this. And it occurs to me that somewhere along the line I screwed up really bad. I made a very poor choice about something and now there's nothing I can do to change it.

PHIL: I think I love you.

KAREN: You haven't even been listening.

PHIL: Of course I have. You were talking about your childhood, right? I love you.

KAREN: No, Phil. I'm really very flattered—

PHIL: I'm not saying it to flatter you, Karen. We're not talking about your drapes. We're talking about this very real and undeniable feeling I have for you. So you're not happy. I think I can sense that from what you just told me. But *nobody's* happy. That's the way things are *supposed* to be. You think I'm happy? I'm not happy, I'm miserable.

KAREN: I am too.

PHIL: I know you are. That's why I feel so close to you. Karen? I can *make* you happy. And you can make me happy. We can help each other.

KAREN: You just said that nobody is happy.

PHIL: I didn't *mean* that. I feel so crazy when I'm with you I don't know what I'm saying. I love you.

KAREN: No—please—

PHIL: I love you. I'm sick with needing you. It's an actual

disease. I'm all swollen and rotten inside, my brain is decomposing, and it's because of you.

KAREN: What's wrong with you, Phil?

PHIL: I'm dying without you, Karen. I'm serious. Has anyone ever told you anything like that? Ever?

KAREN: No. Never.

PHIL: Because no one has ever loved you as much as I do. Jesus, Karen, help me!

(*The* MAN *pops his head through the door.*)

MAN: Excuse me . . .

PHIL: What? What do you want?

MAN: Well . . . my coat . . .

PHIL: In a minute.

MAN: I've been waiting—

PHIL: GO AWAY!

(*The* MAN *shuts the door.*)

I love you.

KAREN: For how long?

PHIL: Until I'm in my grave. Longer. Forever.

KAREN: No, I mean . . . how long would we have to be away for?

PHIL: As long as you want. We don't even have to come back.

KAREN: I was thinking just the weekend.

PHIL: Yes, yes, the weekend. A day. An hour. A single second.

KAREN: I have pasta class Monday nights.

PHIL: Great. Fabulous.

(*Pause.*)

KAREN: I wish I could, Phil. It's not that I don't want to . . .

PHIL: If you want to, just say yes. Don't worry about the rest.

KAREN: I can't.

PHIL: Then just say maybe.

KAREN: If I say maybe, you'll think I'm saying yes.

PHIL: I won't. I promise. I'm very clear on maybe.

(*Pause.*)

Please, Karen. Give me a crumb. Throw me a line.

KAREN: Oh, let me think about it, I have to . . . okay. Maybe. I'd like to—I don't know, maybe.

PHIL: Maybe. Maybe. Thank you, Karen. You won't be sorry. I'm crazy about you. You know that, don't you?

KAREN: I'm not worth it, Phil. Really.

PHIL: This is the happiest day of my life.

(*He kisses her and eases her down onto the bed. He climbs on top of her and starts to caress her. The* MAN *enters.*)

MAN: Look, I'm very sorry about this, but I need my coat.

(KAREN *breaks away and sits on the edge of the bed.*)

Sorry.

KAREN: That's all right. We're done.

MAN: Are you?

PHIL (*rising from the bed*): Come on. Let's get back to the party.

KAREN: No, you go ahead.

PHIL: You're not coming?

KAREN: In a minute.

PHIL (*moving toward her*): Is everything okay?

KAREN: Yes, yes, it's really—Phil, no please, please, just stay away— (*To the* MAN:) Look, I'm sorry, I— (*Turning away.*) Oh God, I hate myself so *much!* (*She runs out of the room.*)

PHIL (*following her*): Karen, wait a—

(*She slams the door.*)

    Shit. Shit shit shit! (*He leans against the door. Silence.*)

MAN: Interesting girl, isn't she? In her way?

PHIL: Huh?

MAN: Personality-wise.

PHIL: How would you know?

MAN: She was sort of my date.

PHIL: Oh.

MAN: But I don't think it's gonna work out. High-strung, you know? I got better things to do.

(*Pause.*)

PHIL: We're in love.

MAN: You and her?

PHIL: Yes.

MAN: Congratulations.

PHIL: Thanks.

(*Pause.*)

MAN: You want to reimburse me for cab fare or what?

(*Blackout.*)

Scene 3

JACK *and* MAGGIE *sitting on a bench opposite a playground in a city park.* JACK *smokes a joint.* MAGGIE, *wheezing heavily, wears a motley exercise suit with race number tied around her chest below a small pin-on button. She has a pair of headphones in her ears.*

MAGGIE: Oh God. Oh God.

JACK: Been doing some running, huh?

(*Pause.* MAGGIE *pays him no attention.*)

    Hey.

(MAGGIE *turns to him.*)

    Out doing some *running*, huh?

(MAGGIE *taps her headphones, smiles curtly, and turns away.*)

    Excuse me.

(*He taps her shoulder.*)

MAGGIE: What?

JACK: I'm talking to you.

MAGGIE: Yes?

JACK: Asked you a question?

MAGGIE: What?

JACK: What's it *for*?

MAGGIE: Huh?

JACK: The race.

MAGGIE: We're jogging against apartheid.

JACK: Really.

MAGGIE: No. Of course not.

JACK: Oh. (*Pause.*) Interesting people, the Boers, you think?

MAGGIE: I wouldn't know.

(*Pause.* MAGGIE *coughs violently.*)

JACK: Something wrong?

MAGGIE: I'm going to die.

JACK: You should catch your breath.

MAGGIE: What I'm trying to *do*.

JACK (*noticing the button on her chest*): May I? (*He leans in closely.*) Ah yes. "Question Authority."

MAGGIE: That's what it says.

JACK: You know—excuse me—that's a bad place for a button. It can restrict your circulation, should I take it off?

MAGGIE: Where'd you get that?

JACK: I beg your pardon, but I didn't "get it" anywhere. It's something I have to know in my line of work.

MAGGIE: And what might that be?

JACK: I'm a cardiologist.

(*Pause.*)

MAGGIE: Please go away.

JACK: Pardon?

MAGGIE: You heard me. I'm not in the mood for it. Go bother somebody else.

(*Pause.* JACK *looks at her and turns away. Silence. Suddenly he leaps up.*)

JACK (*out front*): HEY, JASON! YO! *OFF* THE SWINGS!

. . . YEAH, THAT'S RIGHT! (*Pause.*) I'LL COME OVER THERE! I'LL COME OVER THERE! YOU WANT ME TO COME O— (*Pause. He sits.*) Kid's looking for a brick in the head.

MAGGIE: Cute.

JACK: Yah.

MAGGIE: How old?

JACK: I dunno . . . five, six maybe.

MAGGIE: You don't know how old your kid is?

JACK: Hey. He's not *mine*.

MAGGIE: Sorry, it—

JACK: What do I look like? Come *on*.

MAGGIE: *Okay.*

JACK: I wouldn't have a kid like that. Give me some credit. (*Pause.*) He's my ward.

MAGGIE: Your ward.

JACK: Well, I'm more like his tutor.

MAGGIE: What do you teach him?

JACK: What do I *teach* him? I *teach* him about *life*. Don't play with matches . . . write down phone messages . . . that kind of thing. (*Pause.*) Ah, sorry I bothered you. I didn't mean to bother you.

MAGGIE: Yeah, well.

JACK: It's just you looked . . . in need.

MAGGIE: I'm not. (*Pause.*) What's ten k?

JACK: Pardon?

MAGGIE: Ten k, what is it?

JACK: Well, I think it comes to around six miles.

MAGGIE: Miles.

JACK: It's, you know, metric.

MAGGIE: Six *miles?* I'm gonna kill him.

JACK: Who?

MAGGIE: Nobody. A friend.

JACK: Must be quite a fella.

MAGGIE: He's an asshole. You know?

JACK: Sure. (*He offers her the joint.*) You want?

MAGGIE: No. Yes. (*She takes it.*) What am I doing? What am I doing?

JACK: Well, it looks to me like— JASON! OVER HERE! WHAT ARE YOU, AN IDIOT? HOW MANY TIMES AM I GONNA TELL YOU? STOP ACTING LIKE A MONGOLOID AND GET OFF THE SWING! (*Pause.*) WHAT? WHAT DID YOU SAY? (*Pause.*) THAT'S *RIGHT* YOU SAID NOTHING! Let me tell you, that kid has a mouth like a sewer. I don't know where he gets it from. *I'd* have that kid horsewhipped. You can't do that though, can you? They're delicate, aren't they? There are all kinds of sociological factors involved. You smack them in the head, next thing you know they're strolling through Arby's with a high-powered rifle. And you're to blame.

MAGGIE: Come on.

JACK: You think I'm kidding? Nine out of ten experts will agree with me. Have another hit.

MAGGIE: I shouldn't.

(*She does. They look at each other. Pause.*)

JACK: What's on the phones?

MAGGIE: Nothing.

JACK: It's okay, I'm eclectic. Fred Waring Singers?

MAGGIE: No, it's nothing. Actual nothing. They're not plugged in, see? (*Pause.*) You know how sometimes you just can't stand to talk to someone? You know?

JACK: Your friend.

MAGGIE: It's not enough he's prancing around in spandex pajamas, he's got to keep telling me how *wonderful* it feels to be *alive* on a day like this. And how he feels all this energy, this *beautiful* energy *flowing* out of him. He's like a cheap microwave.

JACK: Spandex pajamas?

MAGGIE: It's his outfit. He's got all these . . . *outfits*, right? He never just *wears* anything. (*Pause.*) Listen.

JACK: Yes.

MAGGIE: He gets his body waxed. I'm not kidding.

JACK: Well.

MAGGIE: Not a hair on him. He's from Portugal.

JACK: Right.

MAGGIE: So there you have it. (*Pause.*) Your kid's on the monkey bars, is that okay?

JACK: He's not my kid.

MAGGIE: Well, your whatever. Christ, I'm stoned. (*She giggles.*) You're not really a cardiologist.

JACK: Not literally, no.

MAGGIE: So are you trying to pick me up or what?

JACK: I'm just sitting here.

MAGGIE: You sit here often?

JACK: I've got a lot of quality time on my hands. (*Pause.*)
    HEY! WHAT I SAY ABOUT HANGING UPSIDE
    DOWN, HUH? REMEMBER JUSTIN HENRY!

MAGGIE: Who?

JACK: That punk from *Kramer vs. Kramer.* You know where
    he falls off the jungle gym? I made him watch it on
    the VCR. Now he wants to be in the movies, are you
    seriously involved?

MAGGIE: Where?

JACK: Your Portuguese friend.

MAGGIE: Yeah, sure. We bought a sofa bed together. That
    counts for something, doesn't it, we both sleep on it.
    (*Pause.*) Ah, my god. He loves me, and I can't listen to
    him speak without looking for the carving knife. He's
    so . . . I mean, just what is going *on?* What are we
    doing? We drift into record shops, we wear nice
    clothes, we eat Cajun food, and what is all that? It's
    garbage, that's all it really is. Absolute . . . Where's the
    foundation, eh? Where's the . . . Look, I read the
    papers. He doesn't know it. The world is coming to
    an end. I'm not *kidding.* We need to be getting better,
    don't we? As a species? We should be improving. But
    we're not. The world is coming to an end and I'm
    spending my last moments thinking about . . . ach,
    who *knows,* sugar cones, skin cream, *nonsense.* Do you
    follow me?

JACK: Yes. Yes, I—

MAGGIE: I don't want to help other people. I say I do but I
    don't. I wish they would go away. Why doesn't that
    bother me? I don't know. I don't know.

(*Pause.*)

JACK: Great dope, huh?

MAGGIE: Yeah.

(*Silence.*)

JACK: You ever see *It's a Wonderful Life?*

MAGGIE: No.

JACK: It's on TV all the time.

MAGGIE: I haven't seen it. It's not a crime.

JACK: Okay, Jimmy Stewart wants to kill himself, right? He's gonna jump off a bridge. Then this angel, bear with me, angel comes down, shows what the world would have been like if he'd never lived. And Jimmy Stewart realizes all the good he's done, without even knowing it.

MAGGIE: Uh-huh.

JACK: Didn't even *know* it.

MAGGIE: So . . . what good have you done?

JACK: Well, there you go. I might be another Mother Teresa, who can say?

MAGGIE: Or you might just be selfish.

JACK: Yeah, that's another possibility. (*Pause.*) I'm going to be finished here pretty soon.

MAGGIE: How nice for you.

JACK: Maybe we could get together.

MAGGIE: How do you mean?

JACK: You know, get . . . together. See what happens. I'm not trying to pick you up.

MAGGIE: What are you trying to do?

JACK: We could just talk. (*Pause.*) Would you like to talk? I think we could talk about some things. (*Pause.*) Listen. I want to talk to you.

(*Pause.*)

MAGGIE: What about your ward?

JACK: I'll drop him off.

MAGGIE: Where?

JACK: Where he *lives.*

MAGGIE: And where is that?

(*Pause.*)

JACK: Well . . . (*Pause.*) It would be interesting, wouldn't it?

MAGGIE: Yes. Very. But it wouldn't be very smart. Besides . . . you're married.

JACK: No I'm not.

MAGGIE: And you've got a kid.

JACK: No, I don't.

MAGGIE: And I think you're just kind of stoned and bored. (*Pause.*) Sorry.

(*Silence.* JACK *stares out.*)

JACK: Look at that kid. I swear he's living with his head up his ass.

MAGGIE: Maybe he'll become a proctologist.

JACK: Yah.

MAGGIE: I'm Maggie.

JACK: Jack. Hello, Maggie.

MAGGIE: Hello, Jack.

JACK: Hi.

(MAGGIE *starts out, turns back.*)

MAGGIE: Um . . . (*She looks at him. Pause. She shakes her head and exits.* JACK *watches her go. Silence. He looks at his watch.*)

JACK: ALL RIGHT, JASON, HAUL IT IN, TIME'S UP.
    ... HEY, DID YOU HEAR ME? I SAID HAUL IT
    IN! JASON, YOU GET OVER HERE PRONTO
    OR I'M GONNA DECK YOU, UNDERSTAND?
    DADDY'S GONNA BREAK YOUR LITTLE HEI-
    NIE! I'M GONNA COUNT TO FIVE, JASON.
    ONE ... TWO ... THREE ... (*Pause.*) FOUR ...
    (*Pause.*) ALL RIGHT, THAT'S IT. I'M CALLING
    MOMMY!

(*Blackout.*)

Scene 4

DON *and* LISA *sitting at a table in a restaurant.*

DON: Would you like another drink?

LISA: No. (*Pause.*) Do you understand what I mean?

DON: Uh-huh.

LISA: So why do they do it?

DON: I don't know.

LISA: Like these men going around with all this, what,
    military shit, you know, zippers everywhere, combat
    boots, flak jackets, I mean people *died* in those things.
    And their heads, they tilt their heads back, just a
    little, looking down at you like, "Hey, baby, you like
    this? I'm *dangerous.* Don't *fuck* with me." Who are
    they *kidding?* Those people, I mean *really dangerous*
    people, they don't look like that. They laugh at peo-
    ple like that. "Hey baby." Come on.

DON: Sure.

LISA: And you see them in the stores, or they're getting their *hair* cut, going, "I want to look like so and so, you know, like a rock star, or a *killer*." Right? Like a *killer*. Why *is* that? Why do they want to look like that?

DON: You mean those guys?

LISA: Yes.

DON: I don't know.

LISA: Do they think it's attractive?

DON: I don't know.

LISA: Am I supposed to fall to my knees?

DON: I don't know.

LISA: Tell me, can't they see how *crude* they are?

DON: Probably not.

LISA: Really?

(*Pause.*)

DON: I don't know.

LISA: Well, *I* don't know.

DON: You want another?

LISA: No. Thanks.

(*Pause.*)

DON: So what do you do when you're not waiting tables?

LISA: How do you mean?

DON: I mean that's not all you do.

LISA: Yes it is.

DON: Well, what do you *wanna* do . . .

LISA: When I grow up?

DON: Yeah.

LISA: I am grown up. This is as big as I get. (*Pause.*) I don't know, I'm taking some classes.

DON: You are.

LISA: Over at the Art Students League.

DON: Well.

LISA: Sculpture.

DON: You must be really talented.

LISA: Actually I'm not. (*Pause.*) Not talented enough.

DON: Maybe I could see your work.

LISA: Maybe you could.

DON: I love sculpture.

LISA: Huh.

DON: It's very rich, very sensuous. Humanistically speaking.

LISA: Don.

DON: Yeah?

LISA: Don't try so hard, okay?

(*Pause.*)

DON: How about another drink?

LISA: No.

DON: Come on.

LISA: No, it's okay.

DON: *One* more . . .

LISA: Are you trying to get me drunk?

DON: Of course.

LISA: And then what happens?

DON: We go back to my place and I show you my flak jacket.

(*Pause.*)

LISA: I know that was supposed to be endearing.

DON: I was only making a joke.

LISA: Who gave you the idea that was funny?

(*Pause.*)

DON: I don't seem to be able to say the right thing to you.

LISA: I'm sorry.

DON: I mean, you were talking before—

LISA: I know. I'm . . . thanks for asking me out. I had a good time. Really.

DON: If you think I'm trying to offend you—

LISA: Yes, yes, it's all right. Shall we go?

(*Pause.* LISA *reaches for the check.* DON *grabs it at the same time. They hold it between them.*)

Please, Don, let me pay for this.

DON: No, I've got it.

LISA: I'd like to. You paid for the film.

DON: This is more.

LISA: Don't be silly.

DON: It's covered.

LISA: Don, please.

DON: I've got plenty of money, okay? You're my date, I'm paying for the fucking check! All right?

(*Pause.*)

> I'm sorry, Lisa. I'm very sorry. You, ah . . . you . . . I
> can't figure you out.

LISA: I'm not that complicated.

DON: We're not really hitting it off, are we?

LISA: We don't appear to be.

DON: I do like sculpture.

LISA: Yes.

DON: I don't know much about it. (*Pause.*) I don't know
what I'm saying.

(*Pause.*)

LISA: Do you enjoy being a man?

DON: It's okay. (*Pause.*) Do you enjoy being a woman?

LISA: Not really.

(*Pause.*)

DON: Would you like to come home with me?

LISA: Only if you let me pay the check.

(*Pause. He hands her the check.*)

(*Blackout.*)

Scene 5

Don's room. DON *sits on the bed in his underwear, struggling to
stay awake.* PHIL *is asleep in a chair, head hanging back.* JACK
stands over him, watching.

JACK: Don. (*Louder.*) Don. Come here.

DON: What is it?

JACK: You gotta see this. Come here. Come *on*.

(DON *gets up*.)

Quiet, quiet . . .

(DON *joins* JACK.)

Look at him.

(DON *looks at* PHIL.)

DON: So?

JACK: Look at his eyes.

(DON *looks at* PHIL *more closely. Pause.*)

DON: Oh man.

JACK: What did I tell you?

DON: That is *weird*. His *eyes* are open.

JACK: It was all the talk of Boys' Bunk Twelve.

DON: You sure he can't see us?

(JACK *wriggles his fingers in front of Phil's face*.)

How can he sleep like that? I mean . . .

JACK: I know. It's a very disturbing concept.

DON: Yeah, it sure is.

(*Pause.* DON *yawns.* JACK *lights up a joint.*)

JACK: So, Don, you vicious party beast, what's up next in our parade of pleasure?

DON: I don't know.

JACK: Twisted sex? Substance abuse? Senseless acts of violence?

DON: Maybe we should pack it in.

JACK: *What?*

DON: Well . . .

JACK: You didn't *mean* that.

DON: That's right, I didn't.

JACK: No, what we're going to *do* is, we're going to have a
    contest.

DON: Why not.

JACK: I want you to reach back, Don, deep into that rav-
    aged brain of yours, I want you to think hard and tell
    me . . . three things that happened in the nineteen-
    seventies.

(*Pause.*)

DON: We already did that, Jack.

JACK: We did?

DON: We did that one like a month ago.

JACK: Oh. (*Pause.*) Did we enjoy it?

PHIL (*in his sleep*): Mom, I'm home.

DON: What?

JACK: Oh, this is great, he's talking in his sleep.

DON: Makes two of us.

JACK: Phil's really a fascinating guy when he's uncon-
    scious. Living next door to him expanded my hori-
    zons. (*In Phil's ear.*) Philip, this is your mother.

PHIL: Mom . . .

JACK: I have something to tell you. You're not really our
    son. You're adopted.

DON: Hey, don't do that.

JACK: We found you in the hold of a Lebanese freighter . . .

DON: Jack, leave him alone.

JACK: Gosh, Mrs. Cleaver, Theodore and I were only playing.

DON: You might be doing something to him.

JACK: Not Phil. He's got an iron constitution.

DON: You treat him like that when you guys were growing up?

JACK: Yes, as a matter of fact.

DON: You ever think he might not like it?

JACK: I always assumed he'd be grateful for the attention. I know I would be. (*Pause.*) Anything on the tube?

DON: There's a guide thing under the clothes there.

JACK: You expect me to touch those?

DON: It's clean, I just haven't folded it yet. Hey, come on, don't start throwing everything around. It's not in the books—

JACK (*picking up a paperback*): *Clans of the Alphane Moon.* Spaceships, how can you read this stuff?

DON: I like it.

JACK (*reading off the back*): "A planet of madmen was the key to Earth's survival!"

DON (*reaching for it*): Come on, Jack, put it down.

JACK (*opening a page at random*): "His efforts to make a sensible equation out of the situation—"

DON: Jack, come on—

JACK: "—out of the situation—"

DON: Jack—

JACK: "—the situation had borne fruit—"

DON: You're *bending* the *cover!*

(*Pause.*)

JACK (*dropping the book*): Nothing personal, Don, but you're one of the most anal slobs I know.

DON: Thank you.

JACK: I mean, it was fine when we lived like this in *college* ... (*He finds the listings.*) Here we are. Let's see, we got, hmm, *Our Tortured Planet* ... *Nuclear Nightmare* ... whoa, tits and car crashes on HBO!

DON: I don't get cable.

JACK: *What?* Are you serious?

DON: I'm not paying to watch TV.

JACK: You gotta get cable, Don. You're showing your age around here.

DON: *Okay,* boss.

PHIL (*in his sleep*): It's like your tongue.

(*They both look at* PHIL. *He rolls over. The alarm clock rings.* DON *shuts it off. Pause.*)

DON: Time to get up.

JACK: Working the night shift?

DON: Guess I set it wrong.

JACK: Don, let me ask you a question.

DON: Uhm.

JACK: Every time I come here, you're always in your underwear.

DON: So?

JACK: Don't you own any pants?

DON: I like to be prepared.

JACK: For what?

DON: Going to sleep.

JACK: Are we hinting at something?

DON: Forget it.

JACK: Hey, if you want me to go don't sit there in your shorts in*sin*uating. Just tell me. Look me in the eye and say, "Listen here, Jack, I'm sorry, it's late, I can *see* you've got *things* on your *mind* but I'd rather go to sleep than sit here in my ratty underwear listening to you." Be honest, Don. Don't get all *ironic* for fuck's sake. Keep me away from irony.

DON: Now listen here, Jack . . .

JACK: Yes?

DON: Have another beer. (*He hands* JACK *a beer.*)

JACK: Thank you. (*He opens it but does not drink.*)

(*Pause.*)

DON: So what's on your mind?

JACK: Did I say something was on my mind?

DON: You hinted at it ironically.

JACK: Don, if you knew anything about me at all, you'd know this: Nothing ever bothers me.

DON: You're lucky that way.

JACK: Luck's got nothing to do with it. It's a matter of style. Image. You have a problem, just ask yourself one simple question: What would Ray Charles do in a situation like this? And Ray, I think, hipster that he is—

DON: What problem?

JACK: *The* problem, whatever problem you're *talking* about, I don't know. But Ray, Badass *Ray—*

PHIL: I don't know, is this my house?

JACK (*of* PHIL): Fucking myna bird in a sport coat here.

DON: What problems?

JACK: You heard the latest? This girl, he's been seeing her a week, every night he goes to her place, right, they talk about the whales or something, he gets to sleep on the couch. She says she's frigid. He says it doesn't matter. She says her uncle raped her when she was ten. He says I love you. She says maybe you shouldn't come by anymore. He says let's give it time. She says I'm screwing somebody else. He says it's all right, we can work around it. Isn't that so *typical?*

DON: Poor guy.

JACK: Calls me up, he says, "Jack, listen, I'm scared to be alone tonight—"

DON: When?

JACK: This, tonight. What am I gonna do, say no? I mean, a friend's a friend. No matter how you look at it. (*Pause. Lowering his voice.*) But I'll tell you something about Phil.

DON: Yeah?

JACK: He's a homo.

DON: What?

JACK: Gay as a coot.

DON: Are you kidding? He told you?

JACK: No he didn't *tell* me, he doesn't even know it.

DON: How do you know it?

JACK: Don, look at the women he goes out with. They eat Kal Kan for breakfast. And *they* all dump *him*. That's not normal.

DON: Is this for real?

JACK: Look at the facts.

(*Pause.*)

DON: Well . . . so?

JACK: *So?*

DON: So he's, you know, so what?

(*Pause.*)

JACK: Exactly, so what?

DON: I mean in this day and age . . .

JACK: At this point in time, yes, Don, I know what you're saying, you're right, absolutely right. Absolutely.

DON: So what are we *arguing?*

JACK: We're not arguing, we're discussing.

DON: What are we discussing?

JACK: We're not discussing anything.

(*Pause.*)

DON: Won't your wife be worried?

JACK: About what?

DON: Where you are.

JACK: Nah. Actually . . . actually she's out of town right now.

DON: Is she?

JACK: Her bank sent her out there, out to, ah, Ohio. Gonna finance another goddamn shopping mall.

DON: She must be doing pretty well, they trust her with
    that.

JACK: Somebody's gotta put bread on the table.

DON: You guys have a great arrangement.

JACK: I thank Jesus every day.

(*Pause.*)

DON: So who's taking care of Jason?

JACK: Well, he's out there with her.

DON: Out there in Ohio.

JACK: It's the kind of place you want to see when you're
    young.

DON: Sure.

JACK: They'll be back pretty soon.

DON: Yeah.

(*Pause.*)

JACK: How's your sex life, Don?

DON: Well, you know.

JACK: I don't know, that's why I'm asking.

DON: It's fine, I'm seeing this girl.

JACK: Well well.

DON: Yeah.

JACK: Well well *well*. What's she like?

DON: She's, ah . . . she's sort of . . . I guess she's kind of
    serious. You know? Very . . . thoughtful. We talk a lot.

JACK: I bet.

DON: No, it's . . . she's always asking me questions. Why do
    I do this, do I say that . . . we talk about how we feel,

about things, and . . . I'm learning to be responsible
. . . and, ah . . .

JACK: Tits?

DON: They're okay.

JACK: Hmm. Well, I wish you luck.

(*Pause.*)

DON: Actually she may be coming over a little later.

JACK: A *little* later? It's fucking three in the morning.

DON: She's a waitress over by the park, finishes at four.

JACK: Sounds pretty devoted.

DON: Well.

JACK: So why you been keeping her a secret?

DON: She's not a secret, she's . . . you know . . .

JACK: A waitress.

DON: She's really a sculptor.

JACK: Does she get paid for that?

DON: Not yet, no.

JACK: Is she in a *museum?*

DON: She just started . . .

JACK: So she's a dabbler, right? She's a waitress who dab-
bles, nothing to be ashamed of. Why don't you say
that, does it embarrass you?

DON: No . . .

JACK: Really?

(*He rubs his face.* PHIL *mutters in his sleep.*)

Hey, you wanna go bowling? That's right, you can't.

DON: What did you mean by that?

JACK: Bowling. Duck pins. Sport of Kings.

DON: About being a waitress.

JACK: Huh? I don't know, that's what she is, right? I didn't mean anything. You wanna go?

DON: It was insulting, Jack.

JACK: I didn't mean it to be.

DON: No, okay, you didn't, but it was. You do that all the time.

JACK: What's this about?

DON: Listen, you could be a little more considerate, all right?

JACK: What am I, your therapist?

DON: Jesus, you're doing it again!

JACK: What?

DON: You're insulting me!

JACK: Oh come on, don't be an asshole.

DON: *Stop* it!

JACK: I'm not doing anything, Don. Why are you getting so excited? Are you under orders? This is not like you. She's a waitress, she's a sculptress, fuck do I care I never even *met* her, tell me—

DON: I feel you really—

JACK: You *feel*, everybody *feels*, *fuck* that. What are you, are you a man? Can't you control yourself? You're *opening up*. You're being *sensitive*. That's a nice *trick*, Don. But don't let it go to your head or you'll wind up getting yanked around by the wiener. (*Pause.*) As they say in the vernacular.

DON: I am not getting "yanked around."

JACK: I didn't say you were, I merely—

DON: Then take it back.

JACK: Okay, I hit a sore spot—

DON: Take it back.

JACK: Please, don't *be* this way—

DON: Take it back!

(*Pause.*)

JACK: All right, Don. Shhh. All right. This is childish. Be
cool. Be *cool*. It's me, remember? Not some lady
you're trying to bring home. We *know* each other. We
know what we really are. We're men, Don. We do
terrible things. Let's admit we like them and start
from there. You want to be a different person? Get a
hug, all the bad thoughts disappear? I'm sorry, it
won't *work* that way. It's not like changing your shirt,
we can't *promise* to be better. That's a lie. What do you
want, Don? Be honest. Do what you *want*. Please. I
beg you. Because if you don't, what kind of ma . . .
what are you gonna be then?

(DON *says nothing.*)

I am your friend, Don. I care about you. I really do.
Okay?

(DON *says nothing.*)

So you wanna go bowling? Hey, I got some amyl, you
wanna do amyl? Don?

PHIL: All my shoes . . . line 'em up . . .

JACK (*to* DON): What you want, Don. Just think about it.

(*Pause.*)

DON: Yeah.

JACK (*poking Phil*): Phil, wake up, we gotta go.

(PHIL *rolls over.* JACK *looks at him.*)

> (*To* DON:) Hey, you wanna see something? You'll get a kick out of this, it's up your alley. (*He hands* DON *a piece of notepaper with crayon markings on it.*) Jason left that. Go ahead, read it aloud.

DON: "Dear Daddy, Mommy is taking me on a jet. We are going to planet light blue. It has a river, and some caves called feeling caves, a waterfall, beds, and slides. There is a city there called 'girls are for you.' I know that is true. I love you but I think I am going to stay here." (*Pause.*) Sounds better than Ohio.

JACK: Yeah right. (*Pause.*) You know, I read that and I thought . . . What the fuck does this mean? Is he insane? What is going on inside this kid's head? I watch him, right, he's this tiny guy, really, his sneakers are like this big . . . but something's going on in there. Something's going on. (*Pause.*) When he was born, did I tell you this? . . . He—

DON (*handing back the note*): She's an artist, Jack. Not a waitress. Understand?

(*Pause.*)

JACK: Yes, Don. Of course. Thank you. I'm glad we could have this little moment together. Only listen, Don . . . (*Pause.*) Don't forget who your friends are. (*He leans into Phil's ear.*) Phil.

PHIL: Huh?

JACK: Time to go home.

PHIL: Go?

JACK: Come on.

PHIL: Fell asleep.

JACK: No kidding.

(*A knock on the door.*)

DON (*getting up*): Oh Jesus.

PHIL: Feel rotten.

(DON *meets* LISA *at the door and blocks her entrance.*)

LISA: Hi.

DON: You're early.

LISA: You're right. Nice legs.

PHIL: I'm never looking at another woman again.

JACK: Very practical.

LISA: What's going on?

DON: Some friends came by.

PHIL: I've done bad things, Jack. So many bad things.

LISA: Sorry to disturb you.

DON: Don't start.

LISA: I only ran over here in the middle of the night.

JACK (*singing*): "Well, I used to be disgusted . . ."

LISA: Are you going to introduce us?

DON: Guys, this is Lisa. Lisa, this is Jack. That's Phil. He sleeps with his eyes open.

JACK: Young Theodore is afraid of the dark.

LISA: Excuse me?

JACK: I said he's afraid of the dark.

LISA: I thought his name was Phil.

JACK: I was making a joke.

LISA: Why?

JACK: In order to be funny.

LISA: Well. So you're the funny one.

JACK: Have we met before?

LISA: No. But we know who we are.

DON: You want me to call you a cab? Jack?

(JACK *walks up to* LISA. *He puts his arm around* DON. *He smiles.*)

JACK: Don tells me you're a very talented sculptress.

(*Blackout.*)

Scene 6

The park. JACK *and* PHIL *sitting on a bench.* JACK *with a child's toy in his hand.* PHIL *looking out front.*

PHIL: I would have destroyed myself for this woman. Gladly. I would have eaten garbage. I would have sliced my *wrists* open. Under the right circumstances, I mean, if she said, "Hey, Phil, why don't you just cut your wrists open," well, come on, but if *seriously* . . . We clicked, we connected on so many things, right off the bat, we talked about God for *three hours* once, I don't know what good it did, but that *intensity* . . . and the first time we went to bed, I didn't even touch her. I didn't *want* to, understand what I'm saying? And you know, I played it very casually, because, all right, I've had some rough experiences, I'm the first to admit, but after a couple of weeks I could feel we were right

there, so I laid it down, everything I wanted to tell
her, and . . . and she says to me . . . she says . . . "Nobody should ever need another person that badly."
Do you *believe* that? "Nobody should ever . . ."! What
is that? Is that something you saw on TV? I dump my
heart on the table, you give me Joyce Dr. Fucking
Brothers? "Need, need," I'm saying I *love* you, is that
wrong? Is that not allowed anymore?

(*Pause.* JACK *looks at him.*)

And so what if I did need her? Is that so bad? All
right, crucify me, I needed her! So *what!* I don't want
to be by myself, I'm by myself I feel like I'm going
out of my mind, I do. I sit there, I'm thinking forget
it, I'm not gonna make it through the next *ten seconds,*
I just can't *stand* it. But I do, somehow, I get through
the ten seconds, but then I have to do it all over again,
'cause they just keep coming, all these . . . seconds,
floating by, while I'm waiting for something to happen, I don't know what, a car wreck, a nuclear war or
something, that sounds awful but at least there'd be
this *instant* when I'd know I was alive. Just once.
'Cause I look in the mirror, and I can't believe I'm
really there. I can't believe that's me. It's like my body,
right, is the size of, what, the Statue of Liberty, and
I'm inside it, I'm down in one of the legs, this gigan-
tic hairy leg, I'm scraping around inside my own foot
like some tiny fetus. And I don't know who I am, or
where I'm going. And I wish I'd never been born.
(*Pause.*) Plus, my hair is falling out, that really *sucks.*

(*Pause.*)

JACK: You know, Phil, in Cambodia . . . they don't have *time*
to worry about things like that.

PHIL: Maybe I'll move there.

JACK: Well, keep in touch.

PHIL: Or maybe I'll just kill myself.

JACK: Hmmm. (*Pause.*) Hey, Phil.

PHIL: What.

JACK: Let's see that smile.

PHIL: Leave me alone.

JACK: Ah, come on.

PHIL: Get *away.*

JACK: Come on, Phil, I see it, I see that smile, come on, come *on*, ooo, here it comes—

PHIL: I'm not *gonna.*

JACK: Yes you are, come on, just a little, just a weensy, just an unsey bunsey, just a meensee neensee, just a—

PHIL: All right, God damn it! I'm smiling, okay? I'm happy, oh I'm so *happy*, ha ha ha! I hate when you do this.

JACK: One day you'll miss me, Phil.

PHIL: Probably. (*Pause. He looks out.*) Well, Jason seems to be enjoying himself.

JACK: Why wouldn't he be?

PHIL: I don't know. He just seems . . . glad to be back.

JACK: I don't see what you're getting at.

PHIL: I'm just saying it's . . . good that . . . you and Carla . . . worked it out.

JACK: Worked what out?

PHIL: Whatever it was. Between you.

JACK: There was nothing "between" us, Phil.

PHIL: Oh. Okay.

JACK: If there *was* something "between" us, we'd sit down and discuss it like reasonable adults. We'd come to an agreement. We'd draw up certain rules, and then we'd follow them. Our feelings don't have to enter *into* it.

(*Pause.*)

PHIL: Well, she's a lovely girl, Jack.

JACK: She is, Phil. She certainly is. And I'm the luckiest palooka. (*Pause.*) So . . . you heard from Don lately?

PHIL: No. What's he up to?

JACK: That's what I'm asking you.

PHIL: I don't know, he doesn't call me. Why would he call me?

JACK: He might be trying to get in touch with me.

PHIL: Why wouldn't he just call *you*?

JACK: Well, maybe he *has,* but I've been busy, Phil. I don't have time to sit around staring at the phone. I have *things* to do. I have food to eat and records to play. I've got places I have to be at and then come back from. I've got miles to go before I sleep. *All* sorts of stuff. (*Pause.*) Darn it, who needs him? Let him play with his dolls. We're having a heck of a time all by ourselves, aren't we little fella?

PHIL: I guess.

JACK: Ho, you bet we are. (*Pause.*) You *bet* we are. (*Pause.*) You know, Phil, what was the biggest mistake we ever made in our lives?

PHIL: What?

(MAGGIE *enters, in running gear.* JACK *sees her. Pause.*)

JACK (*to* PHIL): What?

PHIL: You were gonna say—

JACK: Was I? (*To* MAGGIE:) That's our face!

MAGGIE (*seeing him*): Well, hello.

JACK: Miss, I've never seen you before, but how would you
    like to be a star?

PHIL: Jack . . .

MAGGIE: Might be fun.

JACK: *Fun?* My friend here is too shy to mention it, but he
    happens to be the associate producer of a new major
    motion picture. And frankly you've just saved him a
    trip across the continent. (*To* PHIL:) Go ahead, tell her
    about the picture.

PHIL: I, ah . . . um . . .

JACK: The picture is a modern picture. It's an American
    picture. It's the modern story of American men and
    their modern American women, set against a back-
    drop as modern and American as all indoors. It's a
    spectacle, it's an epic, it's the story of a generation that
    had it all and couldn't figure out what to do with it.
    And it's the story of a girl, one special girl, and her
    quest for meaning in a world she never made. And of
    the man who wouldn't rest until he tracked her down.

MAGGIE: Why would he do that?

JACK: He couldn't think of anything better to do.

MAGGIE: Sounds stupid.

JACK: That's what I say. I keep telling him to make a
    teenage sex farce, but does he listen? (*To* PHIL:) Do
    you listen?

PHIL: What?

JACK: He never listens!

MAGGIE: How's your ward?

JACK: Discreet as ever.

MAGGIE: Good to know.

JACK: How's life at the waxworks?

MAGGIE: Don't ask me.

JACK: Believe me, I won't.

(*Pause.*)

MAGGIE: Mind if I sit?

JACK: Mind if she sits?

PHIL: No . . . I—

JACK: We don't mind if you sit.

(MAGGIE *sits between* JACK *and* PHIL. *Pause.*)

PHIL: My name's Phil, by the way.

MAGGIE: Hello, Phil.

PHIL: This is my friend Jack.

MAGGIE (*laughing*): Hello, Jack.

(JACK *nods.*)

PHIL: You two know each other?

MAGGIE: Do we know each other?

JACK: We don't know each other.

PHIL: Oh.

MAGGIE: Ever feel you're about to do something you're really going to regret?

JACK: Never.

(*Pause.*)

PHIL: Well, hey . . . so you been out doing some *running*, huh?

(MAGGIE *and* JACK *look at each other. They smile.*)

(*Blackout.*)

Scene 7

Lights up. DON *and a* GIRL *in bed. Night. A lit candle sits in a saucer.*

GIRL: Something is coming to get me. I've never seen it, but I know it's there. It thinks about me all the time. One night I'll wake up for no reason and it will be with me. And in that moment I will realize that this is my last minute on Earth. (*Pause.*) Are you still up?

DON: Yeah.

GIRL: I have visions. I close my eyes and see things. There's nothing I can do about it. Once I closed my eyes and I saw a plane going down in a jungle. Inside a boy and girl were sucking on an orange. Their bodies were eaten by monkeys. Another time I saw an old man sitting on a porch. He had just put pomade in his hair. He said, "Mike, clean that blade and stick it in the garage." I have no idea what that was about at all.

DON: You saw this?

GIRL: I didn't *see* it, but I *saw* it, you know?

(*Pause.*)

DON: Do you like working in the record store?

GIRL: I don't work in a record store.

DON: I bought a record from you.

GIRL: I was only pretending to work there. I do that sometimes, go into a place and pretend I work there.

DON: Why?

GIRL: I'm mentally ill.

Don: Oh.

Girl: Does that disturb you?

Don: It depends.

Girl: On what?

Don: Whether it's true or not.

Girl: I used to be a lot worse. When I was fourteen I weighed eighty pounds. I didn't eat. I was trying to make myself disappear. Getting rid of my flesh seemed easy. But I couldn't figure out how to get rid of my bones. That's the hardest part.

Don: I imagine it would be.

Girl: You don't believe me, do you?

Don: I didn't say that.

Girl: What would you think if I told you my father tried to run me over with a steamroller?

Don: Hmmm . . . well . . .

Girl: He was a daredevil. There were six capes in his closet. I was part of the act. He would tie me up and put me in a laundry bag. Then he would come at me in a steamroller. I had thirty seconds to escape. What you have to do is totally relax your muscles. Then the cords slip right off. But my father would tie double knots.

Don: Why?

Girl: He wanted to kill me.

Don: Why did he want to do that?

Girl: Because he wasn't allowed to fuck me.

(*Silence.* Don *looks uncomfortable. Suddenly he gets out of bed and reaches for his shirt.*)

What's wrong?

DON: Nothing. Excuse me.

GIRL: Where are you going?

DON: Out. Don't worry. I just have to go. Uh, listen, the front door locks itself so just slam it on your way out.

GIRL: I don't understand, you're leaving?

DON: I think I . . . um, there's some Hi-C in the fridge, help yourself, okay, and I'll, we'll talk later . . .

GIRL: Have I upset you?

DON: No, no . . .

GIRL: Was it something I said?

DON: Look, I'm sorry, it was nice meeting you, but I don't think . . . you and I should . . .

GIRL: Don't you like me?

DON: It's not a question of that—

GIRL: What did I do wrong?

DON: Nothing. Really.

GIRL: Please, ah . . . please, come here. I know I'm strange. I can't help it . . . Listen, I can tell fortunes. Did you know that? I can. Would you let me tell your fortune?

DON: What?

GIRL: Give me your hand. Please? I know this is upsetting you. I can't help it. Just give me your hand. Then you can go. (*Pause.*) Please?

(*Pause.* DON *gives her his hand.*)

There, yes. That's better. This is very good. Now . . . calm yourself. Clear your mind. Yes . . . yes. Are you relaxed? Nod your head.

(DON *nods his head.*)

> Ah, yes. This is the hand of a man. Very strong. Very powerful. This is a hand that will perform great acts. Terrible, but great. It will hurt many people. But it will seldom be raised in anger. It is the hand of a compassionate man. A man with a large soul. (*Pause.*) Should I go on?

DON: Okay.

GIRL: You feel that you have yet to live. That the years are passing like a dream. This is true. But soon all that will change. People will flock to you. Men . . .

DON: Women?

GIRL: Women, yes. They will be drawn to you. To your power. It cannot be hidden.

(*Pause.*)

DON: How will I die?

GIRL: At sea. When you are very old. Your body will never be found.

(*Pause.*)

DON: You're scaring the shit out of me.

GIRL: Everything will be all right.

DON: Do you work in the record store or not?

GIRL (*lying back on bed*): It doesn't matter. Come here.

DON: I'm not going to be able to see you again . . .

GIRL: Yes.

DON: I shouldn't be doing this . . . I'm gonna get in trouble . . .

GIRL: A man can do anything he wants. I'm blowing out the candle now. Are you going to stay?

DON: Well . . .

GIRL: Then come to bed.

(DON *gets into bed. Pause.*)

DON: Are any of the things you told me true?

GIRL: They're true if you think they're true.

(*Pause.*)

DON: Do *you* think they're true?

(*The girl looks at* DON. *Pause. She blows out the candle.*)

(*Blackout.*)

Scene 8

Don's room. LISA *stands,* DON *sits on the edge of the bed. They are both in their underwear.* LISA *holds a pair of panties. Silence.*

LISA: And that's all you have to say about it?

DON: What else do you want me to say?

LISA: How about sorry?

DON: Well, of course I'm sorry. How could I not be sorry?

LISA: You haven't *said* it.

DON: I'm sorry.

LISA: No you're not. (*Pause.*) I'm going. (*She starts gathering her clothes.*)

DON: Um—

LISA: What?

DON: I, ah—

LISA: YES? WHAT? WHAT IS IT?

DON: I just think you should realize that I've been under a
lot of strain lately.

LISA: I see.

DON: And maybe, I've, you know, handled some things
badly—

LISA: You're under a lot of strain so you go off and fuck
somebody else.

DON: That's unnecessarily blunt.

LISA: Christ but you're a cheeky bastard. Couldn't you
even bother to clean up before I came? Put away the
odd pair of panties?

DON: I thought they were yours.

LISA: I don't buy my panties at *Job* Lot, Don. And I have a
low opinion of people who do.

(*She throws the panties at him. He fools with them and puts them
over his head like a cap.*)

DON: They keep your ears warm.

LISA: You think I'm kidding, don't you? You think, well,
Lisa's just having a little *episode,* it'll all blow over,
chalk it up to boyish exuberance, hit the sack? Who
the fuck do you think you are, James Bond? (*Pause.*)
Did you use a condom?

DON: Huh?

LISA: A *condom.* You know what they are. You see them on
TV all the time.

DON: Wha—why?

LISA: Because you slept with her, and then you slept with

me, and you don't know who she's been fucking, do you, *Don*. DO YOU.

(*Pause.*)

I'm going.

DON: Where?

LISA: I'm going to lie down in traffic, Don. I'm going to let a crosstown bus roll over me because my life is meaningless since you betrayed me. I'm going to my *apartment,* you stupid shithead!

DON: Lisa, it was just a very casual thing. It's over.

LISA: What do I care?

DON: I made a mistake, I admit that, but . . .

LISA: But what?

DON: It made me realize something, something very important.

LISA: Yes?

DON (*very softly*): I love you.

LISA: What? I can't hear you.

DON: I said I—

LISA: I *heard* what you said! You love me! That doesn't mean shit! This isn't high school, I'm wearing your *pin.* You want me to tell you what really counts? Out here with the graduates?

DON: What?

LISA: It's not worth it! Do what you want, it doesn't matter to me. I don't even know you, Don. After four months I don't know who you are or why you do what you do. You keep getting your dick stuck in things. What is that all about, anyway? Will someone please explain that to me? (*Pause.*) Don't look at me that way.

DON: What way?

LISA: Like a whipped dog. It's just pathetic.

DON: Lisa, please. I did something very stupid. I won't do it again.

LISA: Do you have any idea what you're saying?

DON: I'm saying I feel bad.

LISA: I'm sorry, but "I feel bad" isn't even in the running. Not at all. We're talking about faith. *Semper fidelis,* like the marines. They don't leave people lying in foxholes. They just do it. They don't "feel bad."

DON: How do you know so much about the marines?

LISA: It's not the marines, Don. It's got nothing to do with the fucking marines. It's the idea. (*Pause.*) You don't understand what I'm talking about, do you? You're just afraid of being punished. I'm not your *mother.* I don't spank. (*Pause.*) I'm going. Have fun fucking your bargain shopper and cracking jokes with your creepy friends.

DON: Lisa, wait, I have to tell you something.

LISA: No you don't.

DON: I had this dream about you last night.

LISA: How inconvenient.

DON: Can I tell you this? Just for a minute? Please?

(*Pause.*)

LISA: *Start.*

DON: Okay ... okay ... now ... I was ... flying. In a plane, I mean a rocket. It was a rocket ship. And I was all alone inside. With nothing to eat but junk food in racks along the walls—sandwich cremes, Raisinets, boxes and boxes of crap. The smell was nauseating.

LISA: Does this go on much longer?

DON: Anyway I looked outside and there was this tiny planet floating by me like a blue Nerf ball. So I opened a bottle of Yoo-Hoo and sat down to relax. But it must have been doped because it knocked me right out. When I woke up . . . the cabin was on fire! I tried to move but someone had tied me to the chair with piano wire, it was slicing into my wrists like they were chunks of ham. The ship was in a nosedive and I was slammed against the seat. Suddenly, bam, the whole port side blew away. I could see the planet rolling beneath me. A new world, Lisa. Pristine, unsullied. Virgin. I reached out . . . and the ship broke up around me in a sheet of flames. I was tied to a chair falling through the void. My mind left me. (*Pause.*) When I came to I was lying on a beach half buried in the sand. My right hand was gone. The wire had severed it at the wrist. Leeches sucked on the stump. I rolled over and waited for death. And then . . . you rose from the water on a bed of seaweed. On the white sands your hips swayed with an animal rhythm. I don't know why you were there. I didn't ask. You knelt down and gave me nectar from a gourd. You healed me in the shade of the trees. And you never spoke. And neither did I. I had forgotten how. Later on we built a shelter. You bore many children while I caught fish with a spear in the blue light of three moons. And then, one day, we lay ourselves down together on the sand. The breath eased from our bodies. And we died. And the ocean ate our bones.

(*Pause.*)

LISA: What a crock of shit. You expect me to believe that?

DON: It's true. I dreamt it.

LISA: You've got a vivid imagination, I'll grant you that much. Very . . . charming. Very romantic.

DON: It's an omen. It's like a prophecy.

LISA: Of what?

DON: Of us. The two of us, together.

LISA: Well. (*Pause.*) You'd probably make me do the fishing.

DON: I wouldn't. I promise.

(*Pause.*)

LISA: Wait. Wait. This is not it. This is nothing. I can't even talk to you until you tell me the truth. Why did you do this, Don? When you knew I trusted you? Was it her breasts, her buttocks, the smell of her sweat? Was it her underwear? Was it because she wasn't me? Did you have a reason? Any reason at all?

DON: I wanted to see . . . if I could get away with it.

LISA: Why?

DON: Because that's what a man would do. (*Pause.*) Let's get married, Lisa. I want to marry you. I want to be faithful to you forever. I want to put my head on your lap. Can I do that? I want to bury my face in your lap. I don't want to think about anything. Is that okay?

(*Pause.*)

LISA: Would you like to play a little game, Don?

DON: What kind of game?

LISA: A pretend game. Let's pretend you could do anything you wanted to. And whatever you did, nobody could blame you for it. Not me or anyone else. You would be totally free. You wouldn't have to make promises and you wouldn't have to lie. All you would have to do is know how you feel. Just that. How would that be?

DON: I don't know.

LISA: Just pretend. What would you do?

(*Pause.*)

DON: I think I would be . . . different?

LISA: Would you?

DON: I'd like to be.

LISA: Different how?

(*Pause.*)

DON: Well . . . I would . . . I think I would . . . I think
    maybe I . . . (*He pauses and falls into a long silence.*)

(*Blackout.*)

Scene 9

In the blackout, the bandleader's voice.

BANDLEADER: All right, everybody, before you get *too*
    comfortable in your chairs, let's see if we can work off
    a little of that delicious roast beef with some of to-
    day's young sounds.

(*A small, accordion-led combo strikes up with "Beat It." Lights
up on* PHIL *and* JACK *seated at a round banquet table littered
with napkins, glasses, and half-eaten dinners.* JACK *has a row of
soda-filled glasses lined up in front of him. He methodically
pours sugar into them one by one, watching as they foam up
explosively.* PHIL *stares straight ahead.*)

PHIL (*after a while*): Christ, I hate weddings. They're so
    depressing, you know? They remind me of funerals.

JACK: Weddings remind you of funerals?

PHIL: They remind me of death.

JACK: Everything reminds you of death, Phil.

PHIL: No it doesn't.

JACK: What are you thinking about right now?

PHIL: Well, I'm thinking about death. But only because you brought it up.

JACK: I didn't bring it up, you brought it up.

PHIL: No I didn't.

JACK: You said you hate weddings because they remind you of death.

PHIL (*of glasses*): People are drinking those, you know.

JACK: Not anymore.

PHIL: That is so childish, Jack.

JACK: Is it?

PHIL: You don't think so?

JACK: Well . . . (*He pauses and bursts out laughing.*)

PHIL: Why don't you grow up?

JACK: You need some more dope. You'll feel better.

PHIL: I don't *want* to feel better. I wish I was dead.

JACK: You gotten laid lately, Phil?

PHIL: What do you care?

JACK: I like to know my friends are happy.

PHIL: I think that's incredibly tactless.

JACK: Well, I'm sorry you see it that way. (*Pause.*) So you *haven't* gotten laid?

PHIL: You're so curious, yes, yes, I have *gotten laid,* is that okay?

JACK: Yes, that's fine.

(*Pause.*)

PHIL: You don't have any idea what it's like, Jack. You're completely out of it. You've got your wife and your kid. You've got stability. You don't have to make yourself crawl through the gutter to get regular sex. When I think of some of the things I've done . . . it just makes me feel sick.

(*Pause.*)

JACK: Like for instance?

PHIL: Oh, please.

JACK: No, I mean what things?

PHIL: I'm not here to provide you with titillation.

JACK: Yes you are, Phil. You just don't know it. (*Pause. Out front:*) There she goes, the old Earth Mother . . . Hi, honey! No, we're doing fine, we're dandy. . . . Look at her, she's plastered across the walls. One drink and she's ready for pearl diving without a loincloth. She won't keep booze in the house, you know. Jason might invite some nursery buddies in for an afternoon mixer. Not to mention she wants the VCR disconnected, she thinks he needs *more creative* playtime so she bought these toys from Scandinavia, and you know what they are, they're unpainted blocks of wood, you're supposed to have fun *arranging* them. You look at these things and you know why the Swedes keep offing themselves. So I tell her—

PHIL: If you must know, I fucked a girl while she was unconscious.

JACK: Beg pardon?

PHIL: You want to know so I'm telling you!

JACK: You . . . fucked a girl while she was . . . unconscious?

PHIL: Yes.

JACK: How?

PHIL: I deserve to die.

JACK: I'll decide that, Phil. Just what have you done?

PHIL: I didn't *do* anything. She blinked off.

JACK: When? Where?

PHIL: We went out, we came back to her place—

JACK: Who is this?

PHIL: You don't know her.

JACK: What does she look like?

PHIL: You don't *know* her.

JACK: Did she have nice tits? Just tell me about the tits.

PHIL: It doesn't *matter*.

JACK: Just tell me!

PHIL: They were okay.

JACK: Only okay?

PHIL: No, they were fine.

JACK: Good. Go on.

PHIL: So we came back to her place, one of these subdi-
     vided closets, right, and the radiators are howling. It
     was like a pizza oven in there. She pours a couple of
     Scotches, we talk a little. Pretty soon I can tell I won't
     be coming home tonight.

JACK: You bounder.

PHIL: So I get her blouse off—

JACK: Wait, wait, how'd that happen?

PHIL: Just, you know, in the course of conversation. It's
     time to make my move, I take her in my arms . . .

JACK: Uh-huh . . .

PHIL: She keels right over. Wham. Right down on the futon.

JACK: Geez.

PHIL: I'm telling you it was *hot* in there.

JACK: I guess so.

PHIL: Anyway, I tried to bring her around, but she'd had a lot to drink, you should have seen the liquor tab, luckily I was able to charge it—so, I thought, isn't this great, this is just the way I wanted to spend my evening. I was pretty pissed off.

JACK: So you fucked her anyway, huh?

PHIL: No! What do you think I am? . . . I decided to put her to bed. I'd sleep on the floor and keep an eye on her. So I did that, but she was sweating so much, it looked un*healthy*, so I, ah . . .

JACK: You undressed her, right?

PHIL: I took her shoes off, that's all! I took off her shoes, and she had on these tights, so I thought I better take those off too . . .

JACK: And then you fucked her.

PHIL: I had her undressed and I thought, what the hell, I don't want to sleep on the floor, so I got into bed with her, and . . . I don't know. I don't know. I walked home afterwards, sixteen blocks at three in the morning. I was hoping somebody would kill me. I felt like . . . you know what's really terrifying? Everyone's worried about the world getting blown up or something, right, but . . . what if it doesn't? What if it just goes on like this, forever? What are we gonna do then?

(*Pause.*)

JACK: You sly old dog.

PHIL: What?

JACK: What an operator, huh? You old dog.

PHIL: I feel *awful.*

JACK: Ah, come on, Phil, drop the Hamlet routine. Did you speak to her yet?

PHIL: Yeah. She called me. She said she was sorry she fell asleep and maybe we could go out again.

JACK: And nothing about . . .

PHIL: No.

JACK: So? Everything's fine. You had a little fun, you covered your ass, and no one's the wiser. What's the problem?

(*Pause.*)

BANDLEADER (*offstage*): Don and Lisa, we wish you the very best of luck, life, and happiness. This song is just for you.

(*The combo plays "When I'm Sixty-four."*)

PHIL: What did you get them?

JACK: A blender. We had it lying around.

PHIL: I wish I'd thought of that. I bought them a cheese wheel.

JACK: A what?

PHIL: A cheese wheel. A wheel of cheese. It comes in the mail.

JACK: Uh-huh.

PHIL: It's Jarlsberg. Most people like Jarlsberg, don't they?

JACK: I couldn't say, Phil. I know a lot but I don't know that.

PHIL: What the hell, it's not like I see him every day. You catch the bride?

JACK: Yeah, she's a real bowzer, huh?

PHIL: Jack . . .

JACK: What?

PHIL: That's so rude.

JACK: Would you say that girl is attractive?

PHIL: Your attitude towards women—

JACK: Hey, I don't have an *attitude* towards women. I'm not questioning her right to exist. I'm simply asking if you find her attractive.

PHIL: No, I don't.

JACK: So why are you getting upset?

PHIL: Maybe he loves her, did that ever occur to you?

JACK: Of course it *occurred* to me. I'm not an idiot. But that's not going to make her any better looking, is it? So don't give me this attitude bullshit, Phil. I'm just telling the truth. Nobody's going to punish you for telling the truth.

(*Silence.* JACK *moves to pour sugar in Phil's drink.*)

PHIL: Don't do that.

JACK: I'm just *kidding*. (*Pause.*) Hey, you're still working at that place, aren't you?

PHIL: Unfortunately.

JACK: Nine to five?

PHIL: Uh-huh.

JACK: I want you to do me a favor.

PHIL: Like what?

JACK: Like letting me use your apartment during the daytime.

PHIL: Oh. Well, sure. Why not. (*Pause.*) How come?

JACK: Because I need to be able to be alone in the afternoons.

PHIL: What's wrong with your apartment?

JACK: It's no good.

PHIL: Why's that?

JACK: Why do you think?

PHIL: I don't know.

JACK: You don't have to know, you just have to do me a favor.

PHIL: It's my apartment, Jack. I'd like to know what it's being used for.

JACK: All right, don't do it. Jesus.

PHIL: I mean I trust you, but—

JACK: Are you my friend?

PHIL: Sure.

JACK: Then I need your help. I've got to meet somebody and I can't do it at my place.

PHIL: A woman.

JACK: Yes. She is a woman.

PHIL: I see.

JACK: You'll appreciate the difficulty.

PHIL: Right.

JACK: So you'll do it?

PHIL: Um . . .

JACK: Don't "um," Phil, I'd do it for you.

PHIL: That's a little different, isn't it? I mean ... I'm single. You're talking about adultery.

JACK: Oh, please.

PHIL: You and another woman, I don't know—

JACK: Let's not get melodramatic. This has nothing to do with adultery. This is just a nice little affair I'm going to let myself have. A quick tour of foreign panties and then it's back on the bus home. Everybody's happy, no one gets hurt. What could be simpler?

PHIL: I don't think I can do it, Jack. I'd just feel too guilty. I'd be helping you to ruin your life.

JACK: You're joking, right?

PHIL: Did you tell this girl you're married?

JACK: I've implied as much.

PHIL: But you haven't told her.

JACK: Why am I having this discussion?

PHIL: You're so big on the truth, why didn't you tell her?

JACK: Well, we're up on our little throne, are we? You and your fucking sexual sob stories, you think you know the answer?

PHIL: Yes, I do.

JACK: No you don't. Absolutely not. You want to know the *truth,* you want to know what I have *found out* while you sit there twisting your guilt-ridden nuts off? *It doesn't matter!* It doesn't *matter* what you do because nobody is watching, Phil! Nobody's taking notes, nobody is heating up a pitchfork, there *is* nobody there! So don't you dare tell me that I'm doing some-thing wrong, because I decide that, and I decide there *is* nothing wrong. I'm going to commit adultery, Phil! I'm actually going against the Ten Commandments, and as long as I'm careful and don't get caught I don't give a shit. (*Pause.*) Nothing's happening, Phil. Where's the lightning?

(DON *enters in a tuxedo.*)

DON: We can't go on meeting like this.

JACK: Hey, here he is, the man of the minute.

DON: You two look like a couple of derelicts. How you doing, Philly?

PHIL: Okay, I'm great.

JACK: Put 'er there, Don. Big Don. Old Big Don.

DON: Why am I Big Don?

JACK: Because you are, that's why. You look like a waiter. Here you go. (*He hands* DON *a gargantuan joint.*)

DON: Is this for real?

JACK: You can smoke some now and sublet the rest.

PHIL: Congratulations, Don. I'm really happy for you.

JACK: Don't get maudlin, Phil.

DON: You guys having a good time?

JACK: You bet. I love eating next to the men's room.

DON: Huh? Oh, look, I'm really sorry about that . . .

PHIL: Doesn't bother me . . .

DON: See, I didn't know, Lisa did the seating . . .

JACK: No need to apologize, Big Don. I'm sure you had more important things on your mind.

DON: Well, yeah . . .

JACK: You couldn't be expected to bother with these little *details.*

DON: I didn't look too stupid, did I?

JACK: No, not too stupid.

DON: Did you notice when my collar button popped off?

JACK: Actually, Big Don, I did not notice that. Actually I missed most of the ceremony, lovely as I know it must have been, actually since I was not part of the wedding party, that is the wedding party *per se,* I did not actually think it was that important for me to—

PHIL: Well, this is quite a reception. I love the, ah . . . and the *music* . . .

DON: Yeah, Lisa's parents, they're very . . . you know, they wanted a big thing.

JACK: And they're certainly getting a big thing, eh, Big Don?

DON: Ho ho.

JACK: Yep. (*Pause.*) So, Donerooney, this is the day for you, huh. Tying that wacky old knot. Strolling down that goofy aisle of matrimony. Setting down to a big heap o' domestic bliss.

DON: Well, I hope so.

JACK: You're gonna love it, kid. Take it from me. Be fruitful and multiply.

PHIL: She's a lovely girl, Don.

DON: Huh?

PHIL: Lisa.

DON: Well, thanks.

JACK: Big Don, let me ask you something.

DON: Shoot.

JACK: You and the little woman, you're off on a honey-moon?

DON: Uh-huh.

JACK: So what's happening with your apartment while you're away?

DON: My folks are gonna stay there.

JACK: Well, isn't that thoughtful.

DON: Did you—

JACK: Me? Don't concern yourself with me.

(*Pause.*)

PHIL: Well, it's hard to believe.

JACK: What?

PHIL: That we're here, all three of us. And that we've known each other, all these years. I mean we were younger, we didn't know what we were gonna do, or what was gonna happen, and now we're all older, you've got a kid, you're getting married . . . just think.

JACK: It's not that difficult a concept, Phil.

PHIL: I hope you and Lisa will be very happy together, Don.

DON: I don't see why not.

JACK: You can always get a divorce.

(PHIL *looks at him.*)

What I say?

PHIL: He just got *married,* Jack.

JACK: I'm aware of that. I'm just saying it's an option. It's something to take into account. Right, Don?

DON: Well, I suppose it's always a possibility.

JACK: You see? It's a possibility. (*Pause.*) You wanna smoke that reefer now?

DON: You have it. I'm not really supposed to.

JACK: Oh?

DON: I sort of promised myself. It's no big deal.

JACK: No, certainly not.

DON: It's something I've been wanting to do.

JACK: By all means.

DON: Anyway they're just as bad as cigarettes.

JACK: Yet another significant consideration. When do you learn to tie your shoes?

DON: I'm wearing slip-ons.

JACK: The bedrock of a lasting marriage.

DON (*casually*): Fuck you, Jack.

JACK: Does that mean you don't love me anymore?

DON: Not if you're gonna talk like that.

JACK: I thought we were discussing footwear.

(*Pause.*)

DON: Jack, I'm sorry.

JACK: About what?

DON: I don't know.

JACK: Then why did you say it?

DON: I don't know, I thought . . . I don't know, I'm just sorry.

JACK: You know what I always like about you, Don? You're so fucking eager to please. It's really pathetic. (*Pause.*) In a zany kind of way.

(*Pause.*)

DON: I better go. I have to wheel my aunt around.

JACK: Go get her, cowboy.

DON: I'm glad you guys came. I am. Listen, when I get back—

JACK: You know it.

PHIL: Great.

DON: Okay. Rest easy. (*He exits. Pause.*)

JACK: Don of the Living Dead.

PHIL: Huh?

JACK: Guy's walking around like a fucking *zombie.*

PHIL: He looked all right to me.

JACK: Did he? Did he now?

PHIL: He looked happy.

JACK: Phil, and I hate to be the one to break this to you, but you're hopelessly out of date. Happiness, that was the sixties. Paisley trousers, peace marches, that whole thing. This is the modern world. It's kinda young, kinda kooky, kinda—

PHIL: Why don't you shut the fuck up. I'm sick of you and your miserable sarcastic bullshit. (*Pause.*) I'm gonna go dance the hokey-pokey.

JACK: Phil.

PHIL: Don't say it.

JACK: No, Phil, wait, come here. Look at me, come on.

PHIL: What?

JACK: This is bad. This is all wrong. I'm kidding, doesn't anybody know I'm kidding? Look at me, do I look serious?

PHIL: No.

JACK: No, of course not, no, how long do we know each other?

PHIL: A long time.

JACK: Since we were midgets, Phil. Now, all right, we have our differences, our points of *view*, but basically—

PHIL: Yeah.

JACK: Basically we're friends, you and me, friends, yes?

PHIL: We're friends.

JACK: That's right we are, and we're not gonna forget that 'cause of a little— I'm not. I swear *I'm* not. I know what's right, Phil, I do, and I know what's wrong, and . . . so . . . so . . . don't be mad at me, okay?

PHIL: I'm not mad at you.

JACK: You're not? I knew it, Phil, you big hunk, I love you. (*He hugs* PHIL. *Pause.*) So . . . can I have the apartment?

(PHIL *looks at him. Pause. He turns to go.*)

> Phil . . .

(PHIL *starts off.*)

> Hey, Phil . . . Phil! What is that supposed to be, an answer? I'm *talking* to you, Phil!

(PHIL *keeps walking.*)

> Oh yeah? Then *fuck* you. I will *make* my arrangements. And you know *nothing*. Live with *that*.

(PHIL *exits.*)

> You fucking . . . *child.*

(*Pause. He sits. Silence.* CARLA *enters in evening dress. She stands next to* JACK.)

CARLA: Howdy, stranger.

JACK: Hi.

CARLA: Guess what.

JACK: What?

CARLA: I'm having a *good* time. How about you?

(JACK *nods.*)

> Ah, the silent type. I like that in a fella. Wanna get married?

JACK: Sure.

(*She sits.*)

CARLA: I'm a little drunk.

JACK: No.

CARLA: Yeah. I'm just gonna close my eyes a sec.

JACK: You do that.

CARLA: I will. (*She leans her head on his shoulder.*) Did I tell you how nice you look?

JACK: No.

CARLA: Well, I'm going to. You look very nice. I was watching you sit here saying how nice he can look. Why does he look so nice. (*She smiles to herself. Pause.*)

JACK: We should get going.

CARLA: Mmmm.

JACK: The sitter's waiting.

CARLA: Home home. Home with you. Know what I'm thinking?

JACK: Uh-uh.

CARLA: You're not the worst man in the world.

JACK: I'm not, huh?

CARLA: No you're not. I'm afraid you're just not. (*Pause.*)
But you'd like to be . . .

(*She rests against his shoulder with her eyes closed.* JACK *looks out front.*)

(*Fade out.*)

FUN

A Play in Ten Scenes

A NOTE ON THE SET

The set should be suggestive of the various locales mentioned in the text, conveyed through the simplest means. The overall impression of the design should be that of a contemporary industrial landscape.

A NOTE ON THE CHARACTERS

In both dress and manner, Denny and Casper should present the image of two average lower-middle class teenagers, not hardcore punks, heavy metal freaks, or confirmed sociopaths.

Fun was originally presented as part of the Eleventh Annual Humana Festival of New American Plays at the Actors Theatre of Louisville (Jon Jory, producing director) in Louisville, Kentucky, from February 18 through March 22, 1987. It was directed by Jon Jory; the set designer was Paul Owen; the lighting designer was Ralph Dressler; the sound designer was David A. Strang; the property master was Charles J. Kilian, Jr.; and the fight director was Steve Rankin. The cast, in order of appearance, was as follows:

CASPER	Doug Hutchison
DENNY	Tim Ransom
SECURITY GUARD	Nick Bakay
WAITRESS	Lili Taylor
MATTHEW	David Bottrell
LARRY	Dana Mills
WORKMAN	Andy Backer

Fun was later presented as a double bill with *Nobody* by the Manhattan Punch Line (Steve Kaplan, artistic director; Craig Bowley, executive director) in New York City. The production opened on November 6, 1987. It was directed by W. H. Macy; the set designer was James Wolk; the lighting designer was Steve Lawnick; sound design by Aural Fixation; original music by David Yazbek; costumes, Michael Schler; stage manager, John F. Sullivan. The cast, in order of appearance, was as follows:

CASPER	Rick Lawless
DENNY	Tim Ransom
GUARD	Andrew Winkler
WAITRESS	Eden Alair
MATTHEW	Clark Gregg
LARRY	Jim McDonnell
WORKMAN	David Jaffe

CHARACTERS

DENNY
a fifteen-year-old boy
CASPER
his friend, also fifteen
LARRY
a salesman, late twenties
MATTHEW
a movie usher, nineteen
WAITRESS
fourteen
WORKMAN
forties
SECURITY GUARD

TIME

The present. An evening in spring.

PLACE

The outskirts of Roberson City, an industrial town in the
northeastern United States.

Scene *1*

CASPER *sitting on the front steps of a house with a boom box playing.* DENNY *enters.*

DENNY: Dickwad.

CASPER: Hey Denny.

DENNY: How's it going.

CASPER: I don't know.

DENNY: Uh-huh.

CASPER: You know.

DENNY: Right.

CASPER: How's it going with you.

DENNY: Sucks.

CASPER: Yeah.

DENNY (*indicating box*): Mötley *Crüe.*

CASPER: The best.

DENNY: New album?

CASPER: No.

(*Pause.*)

DENNY: So what I miss today?

CASPER: Nothing. Exponents.

DENNY: Shit.

CASPER: Little numbers.

DENNY: You take notes?

CASPER: Uh-huh.

DENNY: Thanks.

CASPER: Sure.

DENNY: Thursday, you know? I just couldn't get into it. My head hurt all morning.

CASPER: Yeah, smoke's coming in off the Monsanto plant.

(*Pause.*)

DENNY: So you doing anything?

CASPER: Nope.

DENNY: Wanna do something?

CASPER: I don't know. My mom's out, I'm supposed to hang around.

DENNY: Where's she out?

CASPER: On a date.

DENNY: Same dude?

CASPER: No. (*Pause.*) What were you gonna do?

DENNY: Have some fun. I don't know.

CASPER: Well . . .

DENNY: You wanna?

CASPER: Sure, I don't know. I gotta be back soon.

DENNY: Okay, so let's go.

(*They exit.*)

Scene 2

The railing of a bridge. Roar of cars. CASPER *with boom box.*

DENNY: This sucks.

CASPER: Yeah.

DENNY: Shit people throw outta cars . . .

CASPER: It's disgusting.

DENNY: PICK UP YOUR FUCKING GARBAGE, ASS-
HOLES!

CASPER: WOULD YOU DO THAT AT HOME? (*Pause.*)
They got the windows up.

DENNY: They got the A.C. on. The *cruise* control . . . they
got dinner on the table . . . (*Mimicking a driver.*)
"Thank God *we* don't have to *live* here . . ."

CASPER: Yup.

DENNY: Fuck *them.* (*Pause. He looks over the railing.*) I mean
lookit that *water.*

CASPER: Okay.

DENNY: You ever look what's in this river?

CASPER: No.

DENNY: You know what I *found* in there once?

CASPER: What?

DENNY: A finger.

CASPER: No.

DENNY: Yes.

CASPER: No way.

DENNY: I did.

CASPER: A whole finger?

DENNY: Most of a finger.

CASPER: Did you pick it *up?*

DENNY: Uh-huh.

CASPER: You didn't.

DENNY: Fuck you, I did.

CASPER: No way.

DENNY: Don't believe me.

CASPER: Whose finger was it?

DENNY: Jesus, the fuck would I know? It wasn't *autographed.*

CASPER: Okay.

DENNY: Some *dead* guy. Some guy jumped off drowned himself in the river.

CASPER: If he drowned himself, how'd he cut off his finger?

DENNY: How?

CASPER: Yeah.

(*Pause.*)

DENNY: Casper, watch out.

CASPER: What?

DENNY: There's something on your neck.

CASPER: Where, get it off!

DENNY: Right . . . there. (*He flicks Casper's Adam's apple with his finger.*)

CASPER: Ah, shit!

DENNY: You wad.

CASPER: That hurt.

DENNY: *Supposed* to hurt.

CASPER: You could of killed me. You could of broke my
wind thing.

DENNY: You'd be dead.

CASPER: I *would* be.

DENNY: Then I could just dump you in the water.

CASPER (*feeling his throat*): I'm practically numb.

DENNY: Bye-bye.

(*He picks up a stone and throws it in the water.* CASPER *does the
same. Pause.*)

CASPER: How far you think we could get on this river?

DENNY: *On* it.

CASPER: Like a raft or something.

DENNY: Who are you, Huckleberry Pinhead?

CASPER: I'm just saying.

DENNY: Geez, bring your camera, you can get great pictures of old refrigerators. (*Pause.*) So what do you
want to do?

CASPER: I don't know. You wanna go to the mall?

DENNY: God, no.

CASPER: You wanna find a party?

DENNY: Who's having a party?

CASPER: I don't know, you wanna see a movie?

DENNY: *What* movie?

(*Pause.*)

CASPER: You wanna find some girls?

(*Pause.*)

DENNY: Let's check out the mall.

Scene 3

The mall. A bench with a large potted plant behind it. Muzak playing in the background.

DENNY: This is fucking *stupid*.

CASPER: Yeah.

DENNY: I hate this place. You know how much time we spend in this place?

CASPER: A lot of time.

DENNY: It's like we grew up in here.

CASPER: They got everything, all right. Anything you can think of, it's right in front of you.

DENNY: People dressing themselves up to look at *shoes*. You count the number of shoe stores in this mall? Lookit Thom McAn, and Kinney, and Florsheim, Fayva, National Shoes . . .

CASPER: Sears.

DENNY: Shoe stores, you hole.

CASPER: They sell shoes at Sears. I got my Ponys there.

DENNY: You know who shops at Sears? Zombies in plaid shirts. They go in there and price band saws.

CASPER: My mother shops at Sears.

DENNY: Mine does too. Is that tasteless or what? She

wants me to wear that shit, I told her to go fuck
herself.

CASPER: You told her that?

DENNY: I would. I will. Her and my father. Right before I
take off.

CASPER: Where you going?

(*Pause.*)

DENNY: Check out that car.

CASPER: Excellent car.

DENNY: Gimme *that* car, man.

CASPER: Is that a Camaro?

DENNY: Looks it. Turbo Cammie.

CASPER: How'd they get it in here?

DENNY: They *drive* it.

CASPER: Camaro's a bitching car.

DENNY: Camaro's the best. (*Pause.*) Know what we
could do?

CASPER: What?

DENNY: Get in that car, jump-start her, tear ass off that
platform all through this mall. Mow these fuckers
down in their Hush Puppies.

CASPER: Except the girls.

DENNY: Crash it through the plate glass, man, bam
through the GNC, bam through the Hickory
Farms—

CASPER: Smoked *cheese*—

DENNY: Bam through the Radio Shack, the fucking Wal-
denbooks—

CASPER: Bam!

DENNY: Then we ditch it in the fountain, right, we break some forty-fours outta Monty Wards, a couple of hunting knives, ammo, and we head upstairs, way up in the mall where no one ever goes, and there is this dude up there, okay, this fat asshole in a control room, all these screens and shit, and he runs the place, he plays all the Muzak and makes the people walk around and smile and buy things only they don't even *know* it, and we shove him down on the counter and blow his fucking brains out.

CASPER (*making machine-gun noises*): Chaka-chaka-chaka!

DENNY: *Except* when we turn around, da-dum . . . there's like eighty security guards standing there with sawed-offs. (*He makes the sound of a safety clicking.*)

CASPER: We go out the window!

DENNY: There's no *window.*

CASPER: Trapdoor?

DENNY: Forget it.

CASPER: Okay, but behind *them—*

DENNY: Uh-uh. We are on our own.

(*Pause.*)

CASPER: What happens?

DENNY: They open up and spray us across the wall.

(*Pause.*)

CASPER (*solemnly*): In slo-mo.

DENNY: *Definitely* slo-mo.

(*They do their slo-mo death scenes with sound effects. Pause.*)

CASPER (*tapping a plant leaf above his head*): This is rubber or something, you know? All this time I thought it was real, but it's not.

(*Pause. A* SECURITY GUARD *walks by and looks at them.*)

GUARD: Evening.

DENNY: How's it going.

GUARD: It's going.

(*He stands there for a moment, then continues on.* DENNY *and* CASPER *watch him go.*)

DENNY: Let's lose this place.

CASPER: Where do you wanna go?

DENNY: I don't know.

CASPER: Okay.

Scene 4

A Big Boy's restaurant. DENNY *and* CASPER *in a booth with menus.*

CASPER: What are you gonna have, Denny?

DENNY: I don't know. Something that's less than three dollars 'cause that's all I got.

CASPER: I'm gonna have a hamburger.

DENNY: So *have* a hamburger.

CASPER: Only I had a hamburger for lunch.

DENNY: So *don't* have a hamburger. Jesus.

CASPER: But that was a Whopper. This is a Big Boy's burger. I don't know.

DENNY: It's the same cow, wad.

(*Pause.*)

CASPER: What are you gonna have, Denny?

DENNY: *Ice* cream, okay? A sundae or something.

CASPER: No, I don't think I want that.

(*The* WAITRESS, *high school age, enters.*)

WAITRESS: Hi.

DENNY: How ya doing.

WAITRESS: Okay.

DENNY: Okay.

WAITRESS: You ready to order?

CASPER: You go first, Denny.

DENNY: Yeah, gimme a chocolate sundae.

WAITRESS: What kind of ice cream?

DENNY: Chocolate.

WAITRESS: You want hot fudge?

DENNY: Yeah, chocolate fudge.

WAITRESS: Sprinkles?

DENNY: Chocolate. Chocolate everything. Make the whole thing chocolate.

WAITRESS: You're into chocolate, huh?

DENNY: I like it, I wouldn't kill somebody for it.

WAITRESS: I would.

DENNY: Yeah?

WAITRESS: When you eat chocolate you're supposed to feel like you're in love.

DENNY: No kidding.

WAITRESS: I read that somewhere.

DENNY: Love is like chocolate, huh?

WAITRESS: That's what it said.

DENNY: Well. Hmm. Yeah. (*Pause. To* CASPER:) You know what you want?

CASPER: Ah ... oh boy ... gimme, um, a stack of blueberry—no, no, give me a hamburger. A well-done burger.

WAITRESS: You want that on a platter?

CASPER: Yeah, actually, are the burgers good here?

WAITRESS: They're okay.

CASPER: Compared like to Burger King?

WAITRESS: Well, they're okay. Is that what you want?

CASPER: Yeah, why not. Gimme that. No, actually, miss, can I have a sundae?

WAITRESS: Chocolate?

CASPER: Okay, yeah, chocolate.

WAITRESS: You sure?

CASPER (*looking at menu*): Actually—

DENNY (*taking the menu away from Casper*): He's sure. He's very very sure.

WAITRESS: Okay, two sundaes.

(*She exits.* DENNY *looks at* CASPER.)

CASPER: What? Should I get something else?

(DENNY *turns away. Pause.* CASPER *drinks his water and begins chewing the ice cubes.*)

Who you looking at, Denny?

DENNY: Nobody.

CASPER: You looking at those guys from Saunders? I don't like those guys.

DENNY: I'm not looking at anyone.

CASPER: Remember we bought those Iron Maiden tees, and they ripped us off right at the bus stop?

DENNY: Uh-huh.

CASPER: I never even got to *wear* mine. How come that stuff always happens to us?

DENNY: Two kinds of people, Casper.

CASPER: Yeah? Which are we?

DENNY: The other ones.

(*He looks away again.* CASPER *chews his ice cubes. Pause.*)

CASPER: So ask her out, Denny.

DENNY: Ask who.

CASPER: The waitress.

DENNY: Get fucked.

CASPER: I don't know, she's kinda cute.

DENNY: You're cute. (*Pause.*) You think I should?

CASPER: I don't know.

DENNY: You think she's cute?

CASPER: She's kinda cute.

DENNY: You think I should ask her out *tonight?*

CASPER: I don't mind.

DENNY: Where you think I should take her?

CASPER: You could take her to a restaurant.

DENNY: She's *in* a restaurant, you bone.

CASPER: You could go miniature golf.

DENNY: Geez, won't *that* be fun.

CASPER: I don't know, you could go walk on the bridge.

DENNY: What are we gonna do on a bridge?

CASPER: I'm just saying you could go for a walk and wind up on the bridge.

(*Pause.*)

DENNY: Yeah, we could do that. We could go to the bridge.

CASPER: I don't mind, Denny.

DENNY: Yeah, that would be pretty decent.

CASPER: I gotta get back anyway.

(WAITRESS *enters with two sundaes.*)

WAITRESS: Here we go.

CASPER: Wow, check this out.

WAITRESS: You want chocolate, you get chocolate.

DENNY: Great.

WAITRESS: Listen, I gave you nuts, okay? I didn't charge you so don't tell anybody.

DENNY: Okay.

WAITRESS: I mean I just felt like it.

DENNY: Thanks.

(*She shrugs. Pause.*)

    So . . .

WAITRESS: Yeah.

DENNY: You like working here or what?

WAITRESS: It's okay.

DENNY: They make you buy that uniform?

WAITRESS: No, they give it to you.

DENNY: That's good.

WAITRESS: Yeah.

(*Pause.*)

DENNY: Umm, how long do you usually work?

WAITRESS: Another half hour. Ten-thirty.

DENNY: No kidding.

WAITRESS: Yeah.

DENNY: Hmm.

(*Pause. She puts down the check.*)

WAITRESS: Have a good night.

DENNY: Oh yeah, you too.

(*She exits.* CASPER *begins eating his sundae.* DENNY *picks up his spoon and sticks it in the ice cream.*)

Let's go. This place fucking sucks.

(*He stands, throws some money down, and leaves.* CASPER *watches him and follows after a moment.*)

Scene 5

The bridge. Roar of cars. CASPER *throwing bits of junk into the river.* DENNY *carving on rail post with a house key. Boom box playing.*

CASPER: I don't know, I'm not doing so good in math. Actually I think he's gonna clip me.

DENNY: Fuck him.

CASPER: Yeah. But it's cool 'cause I'm thinking I could go to trade school.

DENNY: Toolbox U.

CASPER: Yeah, I could learn to do something with my hands.

(DENNY *snorts.*)

That's what they teach!

DENNY: "Boys, today we're going to show how to *do* something with your *hands.*"

CASPER: It's only an idea. I gotta do something, don't I? I mean . . . I don't know. I don't think much is going to happen to me. It's just a feeling I get.

DENNY: Break outta this dump.

CASPER: Yeah, I could always join the army.

DENNY: Right.

CASPER: You wanna join the army, Denny?

DENNY: Sure, we're in the army.

CASPER: We'd fight, wouldn't we? I'd fight, I would. Right?

DENNY: Jesus, Casper, talk about something important.

CASPER: Like what?

(DENNY *says nothing.*)

What you doing, Denny?

DENNY: Carving.

CASPER: What's that, a Hitler thing?

DENNY: It's called a swastika.

CASPER: How come you're doing that?

DENNY: 'Cause I feel like it, Goldberg.

CASPER: My name's not Goldberg.

DENNY: Put another tape on why dontcha.

CASPER: I don't got another.

DENNY: Then turn on the *radio*.

CASPER: The antenna's broke.

DENNY: Let's go riding.

CASPER: How we gonna—

DENNY: Oh, let's just get wasted!

CASPER: You got proof? I don't think—

(DENNY *leaps up and screams wordlessly over the bridge. Pause.*)

   You okay, Denny?

(*Pause.*)

   Denny?

(*Pause.*)

DENNY: Do you have any shit on you?

CASPER: Geez, I don't.

DENNY: I am going to score some shit.

CASPER: How?

DENNY: I'm going to find a *guy* he owes me a *favor* and we're going to fuck ourselves up. That's what I *want*. That's what's going to *happen*. (*He starts off.*)

CASPER: Where we going, Denny?

DENNY (*exiting*): We're *going* to the *mall.*

(CASPER *takes the boom box and follows him off.*)

Scene 6

A parking lot outside the movie theater in the mall. A dumpster sits overflowing with garbage, including several large plastic bags of popcorn. CASPER, *with boom box, rests on one of the bags.* DENNY *leans against the dumpster.*

CASPER (*looking out front; after a moment*): You know, the parking lot looks really beautiful this time of night. I mean without a lot of cars all over it.

DENNY: It's a poem, Casper.

CASPER: Yeah, I guess so. (*Pause.*) What are we waiting for, Denny?

DENNY: He's gonna come around and meet us.

CASPER: You got any money? I only got like eighty cents.

DENNY: It's cool, I *know* this guy. He owes me.

(CASPER *starts eating popcorn out of a torn bag.*)

   Don't eat that, it's garbage.

CASPER: It's just popcorn. You can't do anything to popcorn. (*He finds a discarded movie poster.*) Hey, Rambo, remember Rambo? Check out this gun, Denny. Man, that is *wicked.* (*Imitating a bazooka.*) Ba-doom! Suck on this, slope, we're coming back!

DENNY: You're the slope.

CASPER: Ba-doom!

(DENNY *picks up a bag of popcorn and throws it at* CASPER. *He misses.*)

CASPER: Missed me! You missed you—

(DENNY *clubs him with another bag.*)

DENNY: Stop acting like a child.

(*He drops the bag on Casper's head.* CASPER *"dies."* MATTHEW *enters in usher's uniform.*)

MATTHEW: Yo, man, don't fuck around with the popcorn.

DENNY: It's in the garbage.

MATTHEW: No, no, my buddy's coming with a van, we're gonna sell it to this porno movie on South Washington. (*He picks some popcorn off the ground.*) That look clean?

DENNY: Yeah.

(MATTHEW *puts it in the bag.*)

Matt, you know Casper?

MATTHEW: The Friendly Ghost.

(CASPER *laughs.*)

How's your brother?

CASPER: I don't have a brother.

MATTHEW: How's your sister?

CASPER: She's okay.

MATTHEW: Oh yeah?

(*He laughs. Pause.* CASPER *laughs.*)

Pretty funny, huh? Listen, that's not for free. (*He takes the poster out of Casper's hand. Pause.*)

DENNY: So, Matty.

MATTHEW: Yo.

DENNY: How's college?

MATTHEW: I'm outta there, man.

DENNY: Seriously?

MATTHEW: Waste of my abilities. I'm into venture capital now. Very into the idea of thirty, forty million bucks, my own island, lots of barbed wire, babes, armored Mercedes fleet. I wanna get myself situated before the Dark Ages start blowing back. Won't be too hard. I got a good growth plan.

DENNY: No kidding.

MATTHEW: Yeah, I'll have that in ten years, tops.

DENNY: That's really excellent.

MATTHEW: It *is* excellent. What can I do for you?

DENNY: We're looking for some shit.

MATTHEW: You check the toilet?

(*He looks at* CASPER. CASPER *laughs.*)

This man has a sick sense of humor.

(CASPER *laughs again.*)

DENNY: Yeah, well, I thought you could help us out.

MATTHEW: Uh-huh, okay.

(*Pause.*)

DENNY: Remember Christmas, I did some drops with you, you said come by I wanted anything.

MATTHEW: Huh.

DENNY: Yeah, up in Port Dickinson, I sat in the car.

MATTHEW: *Christmas.*

DENNY: Yeah.

(*Pause.*)

MATTHEW: Okay, so what can I sell you?

DENNY: Well—

MATTHEW: You wanna check out some sens? You want a little marching powder?

DENNY: I thought maybe you could help us out here.

MATTHEW: How you want me to help you? Yo, Friendly, don't sit on the bags. Hmmm? (*Pause.*) You want me to give it to you?

DENNY: You said at Christmas—

MATTHEW: I didn't say I'd *give* it to you. I don't hand out free samples. I'd said I'd sell to you, I don't remember saying anything to you. Most guys, a fifteen-year-old kid—

DENNY: I'm not fifteen—

MATTHEW: I'm developing a select clientele, you're lucky I—

DENNY: We went up to Port *Dick*inson—

MATTHEW: I don't deal up there.

DENNY: Ah, *shit,* man—

MATTHEW: HEY. You *control* yourself. People are watching a *movie* in there, they don't want to hear about your problems. The world does *not* turn around your navel. No. No, I'm sorry. (*He goes. Silence.*)

CASPER: Denny, you wanna go home? It's getting late, maybe it's time.

(DENNY *attacks the dumpster, flinging garbage out of it with his hands.* MATTHEW *reenters.*)

MATTHEW: YO! (*He grabs* DENNY *and bangs him against the dumpster, holding him there.*) The *fuck* is wrong with you? Where'd you grow up, in a cage? Kids, fucking kids, waste my time you don't know *what's* going on. You don't do business this way. Never. This is not how you *conduct* yourself. (*He smacks* DENNY *in the head with the back of his hand.*)

MANAGER (*offstage*): Pauling!

MATTHEW: Yes sir!

MANAGER (*offstage*): You wanna let the people outta the theater?

MATTHEW: Yeah, okay, sorry! (*Pause. To* DENNY:) You're furious, right? Look at me. Furious little kid. You gotta do something about that. You can't go spilling it all over the place. Keep it behind your eyes and don't let anyone see it. You know how a killer thinks?

DENNY: How?

MATTHEW: He doesn't get excited. (*Pause.*) All right. I got some dealing up on Chenango later, you meet me there. Ten-twelve Chenango, across from the sausage factory. Maybe I'll have something for you, maybe I won't. I can't make promises.

(*Pause.*)

DENNY: When?

MATTHEW: A couple hours. Two, three hours.

DENNY: Okay.

MATTHEW: You wanna check out a movie?

DENNY: Huh?

MATTHEW: A movie, I'll walk you in. There's a midnight show.

DENNY: What's playing?

MATTHEW: *E.T. II.*

DENNY: What else?

MATTHEW: That's it. All six movies.

DENNY: No.

MATTHEW: Suit yourself. Hey, give me your radio. Come on.

CASPER: Why?

MATTHEW: Just give it. An exchange. Let's make a deal here.

(CASPER *does not move.*)

> No, okay, it's a favor. Overhead. Remember that. (*He starts to exit. He stops and turns to* DENNY.) How's your father doing?

DENNY: Looking for a job. Waxing the car a lot. Drinking without a glass.

MATTHEW: Huh.

DENNY: Yup.

(MATTHEW *nods. Pause.*)

MATTHEW: Okay, catch you later.

(MATTHEW *exits.*)

CASPER: I don't know, I kinda liked the first *E.T.*

DENNY: It was a fucking *puppet,* you wad.

CASPER: Yeah, I guess. (*Pause.*) What do you wanna do now, Denny?

DENNY: Go meet Matty.

CASPER: What do you wanna do in the meantime? I got eighty cents. You wanna do the Arcade?

DENNY: No.

CASPER: You wanna hang out at the Trailways station?

DENNY: Bunch of alkies waiting for a morning bus.

CASPER: You wanna go to Food World? It's open twenty-four hours. We could look at the magazines.

(DENNY *just stares at him.*)

What do you wanna do?

DENNY: I want . . . to blow up a freight train. I want to hijack a jet. I want Madonna to jump off a poster and come sit on my dick. I want them to drop every bomb there is and be the only person left alive. I wanna be famous, and rich, and I want everybody to be scared of me. That's what I wanna do.

(*Pause.*)

CASPER: Okay, but what do you wanna do *now?*

Scene 7

A small concrete patio behind a house. Chinese lanterns overhead on a string. Card table piled with party rubbish: bottles, potato chip bags, cups, etc. A folding chaise lounge, draped by a plastic tablecloth. Portable phonograph with a stuck record playing at low volume. A child's Big Wheel tricycle off to one side. DENNY and CASPER standing center.

CASPER: You sure this is it, Denny?

DENNY: It's the address he said.

CASPER: There's nobody here. Must of been a party or something, huh?

DENNY: No, it's a car wash. What time did they kick us out of Food World?

CASPER: I don't know. One-thirty. Around one-thirty. Actually it was more like two.

DENNY: Bastards. Who wants to watch some pimply geek stack oranges anyway. (*He begins looking around.*)

CASPER: Maybe we shouldn't be in this guy's backyard.

DENNY: What are you scared of?

CASPER: I'm not scared.

DENNY: Then don't be. (*He looks at record on the phonograph.*) Jesus, *Frampton Comes Alive.* (*He shuts it off.*) Let's have a drink.

CASPER: What if somebody sees us?

DENNY: We're here on business, drain. We got an appointment. Hey, Cutty, my man!

(*He picks up a bottle from the table, takes a long swig, and offers it to* CASPER. CASPER *shakes his head.*)

Come on, don't pussy out.

(CASPER *takes the bottle without drinking. He sits on the tricycle and slowly pedals it backwards and forwards.*)

CASPER: If we join the army, Denny, you think we'd have to—

DENNY (*listening to something*): Quiet!

(*Sound of a woman's laughter from offstage, followed by a man murmuring indistinctly. Laughter from both.*)

CASPER: Where are they?

(DENNY *points toward the house.*)

Can they see us?

DENNY: They're not looking at us.

(*More laughter, voices.*)

CASPER: Well, *they're* having fun.

DENNY: You know what they're doing?

CASPER: What?

DENNY: What do you *think?*

(*Pause.*)

CASPER: You think so?

DENNY: I bet they're down on the floor.

CASPER: Yeah?

DENNY: With a . . . with a *ski jacket* under her ass . . . and her . . .

CASPER: Her *legs* . . .

DENNY: . . . Her legs are open, and she's saying *please* . . .

CASPER: She's not . . .

DENNY: Please give it to me, *please* . . .

CASPER: She's *begging* him . . .

DENNY: No panties, and he's looking down at her . . .

CASPER: Oh God . . .

DENNY: And he says . . .

CASPER: He says . . .

DENNY: He says . . . (*Pause.*) Ah, shit. Who knows what he says. (*He walks over to the bottle and drinks. More laughter.*) Shut the fuck up.

CASPER: Maybe it's just the TV.

DENNY (*indicating tricycle*): Doing that with kids around. That is disgusting.

CASPER: It is.

DENNY: A little kid sees something like that, he doesn't

know what to think. He's fucked up for life. And then you know what, *he* has kids . . .

CASPER: And they're fucked up.

DENNY: And their kids . . .

CASPER: And *those* kids . . .

DENNY: Then *they* . . .

CASPER: It's like a disease.

DENNY: It's like a movie.

CASPER: It's a mess.

DENNY: They probably *are* fucking on the floor.

(*More laughter. Pause.*)

CASPER: I don't think he's coming, Denny. Or else he already did. Or something.

DENNY: Yah.

(*A man's voice comes from beneath the cover of the lawn chair.*)

VOICE: Jesus Christ, who shut off the *music?*

(DENNY *and* CASPER *look at each other.* LARRY, *dressed in a rumpled suit and tie, throws tablecloth off himself.*)

DENNY: Hi . . . ah, we . . . we were supposed to meet—

LARRY (*as Elmer Fudd*): Shh. Be vewwwy quiet, I'm hunting wabbits. (*He gets up, walks to a corner, and starts to urinate.*) This is one of the greatest pleasures known to man. I'm not lying. (*He buttons his fly and turns around.*) Am I right? Now don't *brood* about it.

DENNY: Sure.

LARRY: A *great* pleasure. Pleasure everywhere you look. That's life in a nutshell. And I think you'd probably agree with me, yes? Am I talking English? Hmmm? Am I?

DENNY: Uh-huh.

LARRY: Then why are you *looking* at me like that? Why are you—okay, okay, I know. I've been a bad boy. A bad, bad . . . (*Pause.*) Where is everybody?

DENNY: They're gone.

LARRY: Gone . . . where? Home? Did they go home? They can't go home. You can't go home again, didn't they prove that? I mean, scientifically? Look, I'm sorry, don't listen to anything I say. Just tell me—no, but listen to this—did she go? She didn't. She did. Did she?

DENNY: Who?

LARRY: Who, who I'm *saying.* Sandy. Sandra. The beautiful . . . (*Pause.*) She's gone.

DENNY: Yeah.

LARRY: All right. All right. I'm . . . sure.

(*Pause.*)

DENNY: She left with some guy.

LARRY: Who?

DENNY: Just some guy.

LARRY: *Curse* him. *Kill* him. *God damn* that guy. Yeah. (*Pause.*) Hey. Hey, let's have fun. Let's all just do that. Simon says . . . open up that bottle there. Come on.

(DENNY *opens a bottle of Scotch.*)

Simon says . . . pour three cups.

(DENNY *pours three paper cups.*)

Now drink. (*He drinks his cup.*)

DENNY: You didn't say Simon says.

LARRY: Listen, we're all friends here. Drink up. WAIT. How old are you guys?

DENNY: Nineteen.

LARRY: Nineteen. Great age. Beautiful age.

DENNY: Yeah, I'm nineteen, he's eighteen.

LARRY: Eighteen, a great age.

DENNY: The best.

LARRY: He doesn't *say* much.

DENNY: He likes to think.

LARRY: Who doesn't. What it *is,* man.

CASPER: Hi.

LARRY: So here we *are,* three really *happening* dudes, we're young, we're— (*Pause. He looks at them closely.*) Oh boy. I'm sorry. I can't believe the way I'm acting. Look at you two. Of *course* you are. I can't *believe* it. (*Pause.*) You don't remember me, do you?

DENNY: Ah . . .

LARRY: You don't, you don't! I can't believe it. I remember *you.* You're Michael and you're, um . . . Jeffrey.

CASPER: Casper.

LARRY: Casper, sure, sure. *Look* at you guys. You must be what, eighteen, nineteen by now, right?

DENNY: Right.

LARRY: And you don't remember Larry? I'm hurt, I'm hurt!

DENNY: You know, I think . . .

LARRY: Oh, come on, remember me and Sandy? Remember, I used to come around when you guys lived over on, what, Murray Street, geez, must be ten years.

DENNY (*with a look to* CASPER): Larry, sure.

LARRY: Oh, fellas, your sister, your sister, I can't apologize eno— You *know* me, I wouldn't . . . but God she looked great tonight, she really . . . she left with some guy, you know that?

DENNY: No.

LARRY: She did, some guy. I had a little drinks, I admit it, but I mean Sandy, ten years, I just *remembered* . . . (*Pause.*) Yeah. Little Mikey and Jeffy. Little kids. How come you guys grew up, and I'm not any older?

DENNY: I don't know, Larry, it's hard to say.

LARRY: It is, it's hard. It really is. (*Pause.*) Well, fuck it. Let's have some fun. Let's just do that.

DENNY: Okay.

LARRY: I mean what are we here for anyway? The night *beckons.* It's just out there beckoning away, huh? What do you wanna do?

DENNY: Us three?

LARRY: Damn straight. These bozos don't know the meaning of party. What do you want?

DENNY: Ah . . .

LARRY: You name it. Tell me. *Anything* you want to do.

DENNY: Anything?

LARRY: Anything. My little *buddies.*

(*Pause.*)

DENNY: Well, frankly, Larry . . . we'd like to get laid.

LARRY: I also would like to get laid.

DENNY: So would we.

LARRY: The question is, how low are your standards?

DENNY: Pretty low.

LARRY: You guys been to Watsonville lately?

DENNY: Yeah.

LARRY: You been on Nanticoke Avenue?

DENNY: Uh-huh.

LARRY: You been in the whorehouse behind the Power Test?

DENNY: No.

LARRY: Then, gentlemen, Paradise awaits.

DENNY: Only we don't got any money, Larry.

LARRY: No no. No money. My treat. Mikey and Jeffy. Little buddies. You just tell Sandra I . . . you say your main man Larry . . . you tell her . . . you just let her know.

DENNY: Okay.

LARRY: So . . . LET'S DO IT!

(*He beats his chest, Tarzan-like, grabs a bottle, and runs off.* DENNY *starts to follow.*)

CASPER: Denny, I—

DENNY: Shut up. We're finally gonna have some *fun!*

(*He exits.* CASPER *gets his boom box and follows.*)

Scene 8

Larry's car. CASPER *in back.* DENNY *in front with* LARRY, *who is driving very fast. The opening chords of Springsteen's "Born to Run" boom out of the car speakers.*

LARRY: BROOOO-*OOCE!* (*He sings along for a few lines, getting the words wrong. He takes a drink from the bottle and passes it to* DENNY.) This is GREAT. Isn't it? Isn't this just GREAT? Gimme a car, man! Gimme a *road!* (*Sticking his head out the window.*) *Ba-ROOOOOO-OOCE!*

DENNY: Nice car, Larry.

LARRY: Isn't it? Isn't it GREAT? It's the greatest car! I *live* in this car. I mean I *sleep* in motels but I live in *this car.* And it's not even mine! It isn't! They *give* it to me! For my *job!* I could wreck it if I want! Just squash it flat! (*He laughs and takes his hands off the wheel.*) BROOO-*OOCE!* (*He puts his hands back. Pause.*) It's a great country, fellas. Isn't it a great country?

DENNY: The greatest, Larry.

LARRY (*turning the music down slightly*): No, no, I'm serious. I am. You can say what you want about it, but here it is, all of it, it's *right here.* The land . . . the people . . . the *garbage.* Our garbage is the best garbage in the world, I don't *care* what they say I love it. Now you *been* to California, Mikey.

DENNY: No.

LARRY: Oh, we all have to go to California, we have to! Everybody's young in California, it's not like here. There's *nothing* here, it's all worn out. I mean . . . you take a guy like me, huh? Right?

DENNY: Yeah.

LARRY: Let's take a guy who— (*He swerves the wheel suddenly.*) Whoa, that was a fucking bump, did you see that? You okay there, Jeff?

CASPER: I'm fine.

LARRY: All right, a guy who, let's be honest, I had opportunities, *great* opportunities, and I threw them *away.* I had—I did very well on my SATs, you know that, very well, the top of the percent—*experts* told me things and I just did not listen, because *I* thought . . . I thought I *deserved* . . . well, fuck what I *thought.* Here it is, right here. I'm selling industrial tubing out of a rented car. Is that a disgrace? Is it?

DENNY: Um . . .

LARRY: I make a lot of money, thank you, I do very well indeed. You march in there and turn it around, that's business. And there's no reason you can't— (*He swerves again.*) Whoa, sorry, sorry—you can't come back home and feel . . . something. Just . . . something. What I'm saying is . . . hey, guess how old I am.

DENNY: I don't know, Larry.

LARRY: Guess!

DENNY: You're, ah—

LARRY: No, no, not you. Jeffy, Jeffy!

CASPER: Thirty-five?

LARRY: What? Jesus, no! I'm twenty-nine—twenty-eight. I'm your age. Well, not—but you know. Rock and *roll!* Hey, remember I took you guys to go-karts, you, me, and Sandy? You were scared to get on? Does your sister ever talk about me? So who was that guy? No, don't tell me.

(*Pause. They drive in silence.*)

DENNY: Where we going, Larry?

LARRY: Huh?

DENNY: We're going to Watsonville, right?

LARRY: Oh, we're gonna have fun.

DENNY: Isn't it the other way?

(*Pause.*)

LARRY: Right, yeah . . . Oh, but we're going to the motel first. I need some cash. These ladies don't come cheap. Actually I don't think they come at all. But they fake it pretty good. Huh?

DENNY: Sure.

LARRY: You *know* what I'm saying.

DENNY: Ah, Larry—

LARRY: The sweet spot, boys, it's just like coming home.

DENNY: Larry—

LARRY: Hey, you think they take credit cards? Maybe I could—

CASPER (*covering his face*): WATCH OUT!

LARRY: What the—

(*He swerves the car violently and slams the brakes. They plunge forward in their seats as the car stops. Silence.*)

DENNY: Jesus Christ.

LARRY: Son of a bitch.

DENNY: You okay?

CASPER: Uh-huh.

LARRY: Who put that asshole behind a wheel?

DENNY: You were on the wrong side of the *road,* Larry.

LARRY: No I wasn't. Was I?

DENNY: You almost got us killed!

(*Pause.*)

LARRY: Ah . . . yeah . . . whoo. You know what it is, it's these rented cars. You take your life in your hands, they don't care. I tell you what, let's just, I just need to

. . . (*He takes a drink from the bottle.*) Yeah, yeah, I'm just gonna take a second here and get my bearings, and then we'll—okay, I'm fine. I am. Actually I think I was supposed to be in Albany tonight, I don't know why I . . . (*He puts his head down and starts sobbing.*) Oh God . . . what am I doing here . . . my whole life . . . I want to be a baby, that's all . . . I just wanna be a baby . . .

(*He cries some more, then becomes quiet. Pause.*)

DENNY: Larry? You okay?

(*He shakes him tentatively.* LARRY *does not stir.* DENNY *leans him against the seat. Larry's head drops back, mouth open.*)

CASPER: Is he dead?

DENNY: He's asleep. Do you believe this guy?

CASPER: He drank too much.

DENNY: He's a fucking *basket* case. No wonder that girl dumped him. God, I don't wanna get old. Yo, wake up! (*No response from* LARRY.) Can you drive?

CASPER: I'm not allowed.

DENNY: *Can* you?

CASPER: Not a stick.

DENNY (*turning off the tape deck*): What *is* this shit?

(*Pause.*)

CASPER: Are we having fun now, Denny?

(DENNY *pays him no attention. He is staring hard at* LARRY.)

    What you looking at?

DENNY: Nothing much.

CASPER: So?

(*Pause.*)

DENNY: You know what we could do?

CASPER: What?

DENNY: We could . . . just . . .

CASPER: What?

(DENNY *reaches over and puts his hand on Larry's exposed throat. He strokes it gently. He looks at* CASPER, *smiling.* CASPER *laughs briefly.* DENNY *puts his thumb and forefinger over Larry's Adam's apple. He presses it slightly.* LARRY *grunts. He wraps his hand around Larry's throat.* LARRY *grunts again without waking.*)

(*Reaching forward.*) Okay, Denny—

(DENNY *slaps him away with his other hand. He increases the pressure for several seconds. Suddenly* LARRY *coughs and wakes.* DENNY *takes his hand away.* LARRY *looks at them, dazed. Pause.*)

LARRY: What happened?

DENNY: You fell asleep.

LARRY: I did?

DENNY: Yah.

(*Pause.* LARRY *clears his throat.*)

You still wanna go to the motel?

LARRY: Motel?

DENNY: You said for money.

LARRY: Money, right. No problem. And we're going to . . .

DENNY: Watsonville.

LARRY: Right, Watsonville. (*Remembering.*) Watsonville, yeah! (*Pause.*) What's the car doing in a ditch?

(*He looks at them and bursts out laughing. He turns on the tape deck, loud, and floors the pedal. They lurch forward in their seats.*)

THIS IS FUCKING GREAT!

Scene 9

The upper terrace of a motel off the highway. DENNY *and* CASPER *in front of a door.*

DENNY: You sure this is his room?

CASPER: I thought I saw him go up here.

DENNY (*looking along the terrace*): Christ, this place is built like a *dog* kennel. (*He leans into the door.*) Larry . . . Hey, Larry . . . What the fuck is he doing in there?

CASPER: He probably fell asleep.

DENNY: *Larry* . . . Shit, this isn't his room. Go down the office and ask the guy the room he's in.

CASPER: What should I ask him?

DENNY: Larry's fucking room!

CASPER: Larry *who?*

DENNY: Larry the fuck I don't know what his name is!

(*Pause.*)

CASPER: There's nobody down there anyway, Denny. It's too late.

DENNY (*pounding on the doorway*): WAKE UP! (*Pause.*) Where are we?

CASPER: I don't know. Up the Thruway somewhere. I wish I had like another shirt or something. It's getting

kind of cold. It's weird, you know, in the daytime it's
hot and then—

DENNY: He said he was going to get us *laid.*

CASPER: Yeah.

DENNY: He was gonna take us and he was gonna *pay* for it!
He *promised!*

CASPER: Well, that would of been nice.

DENNY: *Nice?* Don't you *want* it?

CASPER: It just didn't work out.

DENNY: No. Shit. He *promised.* We could be getting ourselves blown right now—

CASPER: I don't—

DENNY: We could! Right now by some *whore* with *big* tits.
She'd *have* to, whatever we want!

CASPER: No she wouldn't.

DENNY: Bull*shit* she would, it's her job. I'd say go down on
me and she'd do it!

CASPER: Come on, stop.

DENNY: Like a fucking *Tootsie* pop . . .

CASPER: Oh geez . . .

DENNY: Right on me the whole night! (*Pause.*) Ah, how
come I got to feel all this shit when there's nothing I
can do about it? Why can't I get just ONE FUCKING
THING?

(*Pause.*)

CASPER: We could . . . jerk off.

DENNY: What?

CASPER: You know. Like in the Scouts.

DENNY: Are you sick?

CASPER: There's no one around.

DENNY: Me! I'm around! I don't wanna watch you humping your knuckles!

CASPER: I was only saying.

DENNY: Fucking disgusting! (*Pause.*) All right. But don't look at me.

CASPER: Huh?

DENNY: Don't *look* at me! Turn around. Come on, let's just get it over with!

(*They stand with their backs to each other, unzip their pants, put their hands down their shorts, and begin to masturbate.*)

(*Stopping.*) What the fuck am I doing?

CASPER: I don't know, Denny.

(*They take their hands out of their pants.*)

Have you done it yet? With a girl?

DENNY: Yeah.

CASPER: Is it fun?

DENNY: It's a riot. (*Pause.*) Let's get outta here.

CASPER: We don't know where we are.

DENNY: Then it doesn't matter where we go.

CASPER: I guess not.

(DENNY *looks at* CASPER. *Pause. He takes off his jacket.*)

DENNY: Here.

(*He throws him the jacket.* CASPER *catches it.* DENNY *exits.*)

Scene 10

A concrete pillar beneath a highway overpass, covered with graffiti. Various kinds of junk shored up against the foot of the pillar, including a cushionless sofa, a broken armchair, and a discarded oven. Sound of steady rain mixed with the rumble of tractor-trailers passing by overhead. DENNY *and* CASPER *stand with wet hair and rain-splattered clothes. They look out at the rain.*

CASPER (*after a moment*): Well, maybe we *shoulda* walked the other way.

DENNY: Great idea.

CASPER: I just thought that gas station looked familiar . . . I don't know. At least it's dry under here.

DENNY: It's perfect.

CASPER: April showers bring . . . what do they bring, Denny?

DENNY: Earthworms. Earthworms coming up all over the sidewalks. (*Taking off his wet T-shirt.*) Yach! (*He throws it off to the side, leaving him bare chested.*)

CASPER: Here, Denny, take your coat back.

DENNY: Uh-uh.

CASPER: Come on, you'll get froze.

DENNY: I don't *want* it.

(*Pause.*)

CASPER: You know what the Indians up here used to do? When they were like out in the forest at night? They'd dig a hole in the ground, then they'd lie down and cover themselves with leaves. It kept them warm. Only I don't see any leaves around.

DENNY: You don't see many Indians either.

CASPER: No, you don't.

DENNY (*moving to sofa*): I'm gonna lie down.

CASPER: Smells of piss.

DENNY: All the comforts of home.

(*He stretches himself out on the sofa.* CASPER *looks inside the oven and takes out a pile of old magazines. He sits in the armchair and starts thumbing through them.*)

What's that?

CASPER (*looking at cover*): *Family Circle.* December 1979.

(*Pause.*)

DENNY: Read me something.

CASPER: Like what?

DENNY: I don't care. Just read it out loud.

(CASPER *picks a page at random.*)

CASPER (*speaking haltingly, without punctuation*): "One-oh-one ideas for Christmas fun holiday time is a time of family joy but today's mother can find her hands full when it comes to keeping the kids . . . okewped but with a little bit of—"

DENNY: What?

CASPER: "With a little—"

DENNY: Keeping them *what?*

CASPER: Okewped. (*Pause.*) Osapeed?

(DENNY *takes the magazine from him and looks at it.*)

DENNY: Jesus. *Occupied.* Keeping the kids *occupied.*

CASPER: Oh, yeah.

DENNY: Don't you *know* that word?

CASPER: Sure.

DENNY: That's not a hard word! It's right there! Occupied! Can't you read even?

CASPER: Yeah, I can read. I can read fine. I just need some time to . . . sound out the words. (*Pause.*) Should I do some more?

(DENNY *shakes his head and lies back down. A truck goes by overhead.*)

DENNY: Oh God will you shut UP! Somebody's trying to sleep!

CASPER: They're sixty feet up, Denny. They don't know we're here.

DENNY: But we are. Whether they like it or not. I'm here.

CASPER: Come on, Denny, take your jacket.

DENNY: Casper . . . are you real?

CASPER: Huh? Ah . . . I guess so. I'm real. Am I?

(DENNY *looks at him. Pause.*)

DENNY: Yeah. You're lucky.

(*Sound of a man whistling in the distance.* DENNY *leans forward and whispers.*)

   Cop?

CASPER: I don't know. (*He looks off.*) Doesn't look it.

DENNY: Alone?

CASPER: Uh-huh.

DENNY: Big dude?

CASPER: It's hard to tell. (*Pause.*) Should we . . . ask him for directions?

DENNY (*not listening*): Huh?

CASPER: Directions home, Denny. I mean he doesn't look like a—

DENNY: Yeah. Yeah, good idea. You ask him for directions. I'll stash myself here. When he stops I'll yoke him up from the back.

CASPER: What?

DENNY: Like this. (*He demonstrates with his twisted-up T-shirt, miming wrapping it around someone's neck and pulling it taut.*) Right?

CASPER: Aw, Denny.

DENNY: We're not gonna hurt him. We're just gonna do him. We can take a taxi home!

CASPER: No, Denny, why?

DENNY: Because I *want* to, okay? Because I fucking feel like it!

CASPER: Oh boy. Oh no. Oh geez.

DENNY: You gonna help me or not?

(CASPER *does not answer.*)

> Then get outta here. I'm gonna bag this chump and you're a fucking chickenshit, you are. They won't *take* you in the army. Fuck off!

(*Pause.*)

CASPER: What do I have to do?

DENNY: Okay. Okay. Ask him . . . what time it is. Go in for his wallet while I hold him. Don't act stupid.

(*He ducks behind the sofa.* CASPER *sits in the chair and waits. A* WORKMAN *in overalls and raincoat enters.* CASPER *rises.*)

CASPER: Excuse me, sir, can you tell me what's the time?

(*Pause.*)

WORKMAN: It's around five-thirty.

CASPER: Okay, thanks. (*Pause.*) Does this lead back to
    town?

WORKMAN: Service road to the coal dump.

(*Pause.*)

CASPER: Listen . . . I think you should—

(DENNY *comes up behind the* WORKMAN *and twists the T-shirt
around his neck. The* WORKMAN *lurches forward.* DENNY *tries
to drag him back. They stand like this for a few seconds. Then the*
WORKMAN *starts inching forward.*)

DENNY: His wallet!

(CASPER *does not move.*)

    The fucking wallet! What are you—

(*The* WORKMAN *drops suddenly and tosses* DENNY *over onto
the ground. He kicks him twice. He looks at* CASPER, *who
remains still. He moves to kick* DENNY *again.* DENNY *cringes.
The* WORKMAN *lowers his foot. Pause.*)

WORKMAN: Cocksucking little punks. Fence you off in a
    desert somewhere so you can all beat your own brains
    out. I worked all my life. You try it!

(*He glares at them for a moment and stalks off.* CASPER *watches
him go, then comes over to* DENNY.)

CASPER: You all right, Denny? Let me—

(DENNY *waves him away.*)

    We gotta go, Denny. He might call the police.

(DENNY *doesn't move.*)

    Can you walk?

DENNY (*in an even tone*): Where were you?

CASPER: I was here. I was standing.

DENNY: Why didn't you do something? (*Pause.*) You're not saying anything.

CASPER: I couldn't. I didn't want to.

DENNY: How come?

CASPER: It's wrong, Denny. It's just wrong to do.

DENNY: The *fuck* made you an expert!

CASPER (*coming up to him*): Oh, I don't know, let's go be-fore—

DENNY (*pushing him back*): Stay . . . away . . . from me. 'Cause I swear to God I wanna kill some fucking thing. (*With a yell he lunges at the oven and yanks at its door until he tears it off. He charges up to the pillar and starts pounding the door against it.*) You, fucker! I want you to die, God damn you! You fucking *highway* . . . you fucking *bridges* . . . and *cities* and houses and all the people crawling in 'em, I don't WANT you here! I don't want you in my HEAD! Get OUT! GET OUT GET OUT GET OUT! (*He throws down the door, nearly exhausted. He sees Casper's radio.*) And *this* . . . this is just *crap* . . . (*He picks it up and lifts it over his head.*)

CASPER: Don't break it, Denny.

DENNY: WHY NOT!

CASPER: 'Cause it's mine. 'Cause I need it. 'Cause we're friends. And 'cause . . . it's not gonna make any dif-ference.

(*Pause. DENNY feigns tossing the radio against the pillar and throws it sharply at CASPER, who catches it. He takes a last swipe at the sofa and collapses onto it. Pause. A police siren sounds in the distance, then fades away.*)

DENNY: Jesus, can't I even get arrested?

CASPER: Not this time I guess. (*He picks up the radio and wipes it clean with the edge of his shirt.*) It's getting light. I shoulda been back a while ago. It's a long walk home.

DENNY: Well . . . at least it's Saturday.

CASPER: It's Friday, Denny. Friday morning.

DENNY: Oh good.

(*Pause.*)

CASPER: Hey, we had some fun tonight, didn't we? I mean . . . all the other stuff aside. We had a little fun.

DENNY: Yeah.

CASPER: Yeah, we had some fun. (*Pause.*) So, Denny . . . what do you wanna do now?

(DENNY *looks straight out. He draws in a long, slow breath and holds it.*)

(*The lights fade to black.*)

NOBODY

Nobody was originally presented at the 1987 National Playwrights Conference at the Eugene O'Neill Theatre Center.

Nobody was later presented as a double bill with *Fun* by the Manhattan Punch Line (Steve Kaplan, artistic director; Craig Bowley, executive director) in New York City. The production opened on November 6, 1987. It was directed by W. H. Macy; the set designer was James Wolk; the lighting designer was Steve Lawnick; sound design by Aural Fixation; original music by David Yazbek; costumes, Michael Schler; stage manager, John F. Sullivan. The cast, in order of appearance, was as follows:

CARL	John Christopher Jones
SUPERVISOR	Joe Jamrog
WALTER	Frank Hamilton
CATHY	Beth McDonald
DENNY	Tim Ransom
TED	Michael Hume
JEANETTE	Sophie Hayden
JIM	Vasili Bogazianos
BOBBY	David Jaffe
SALESMAN	Jim McDonnell
BARTENDER	Joe Jamrog
PSYCHIATRIST	David Jaffe
WORKER	Vasili Bogazianos

Desires still remain extraordinarily high, while the means of satisfying them are diminished day by day.

> Tocqueville
> *Democracy in America*

CHARACTERS

CARL
a man in his thirties
CATHY
his wife
DENNY
their son, fifteen
TED
a neighbor
JEANETTE
his wife
WALTER [MAN in bar]
an unemployed man
BOBBY
an unemployed man
JIM
an unemployed man
SUPERVISOR
PSYCHIATRIST
SALESMAN
BARTENDER
WORKER

TIME

The present. Over the course of several weeks.

PLACE

Various locations around Roberson City, an industrial town in the northeastern United States.

Scene 1

An office. Supervisor *behind desk.* Carl *seated in chair.*

Supervisor: Yadda yadda yadda. All this bullshit.

(Carl *lets out a breath. Pause.*)

>Carl, I am just as sorry as can be.

Carl: Appreciate it.

Supervisor: This is the worst part of my job. People think this is *easy,* let *them* sit here. Call me at home.

Carl: I wouldn't want to be in your shoes.

Supervisor: And I could name you ten other guys I'd rather be saying this to. But I don't get that choice. I get this, I *do* this.

(*He shows* Carl *a computer printout.* Carl *looks at it without expression. Pause.*)

Carl: Well. You have to do what they tell you.

Supervisor: Sad truth, Carl. You couldn't get anything done *otherwise.*

Carl: I've never been fired before.

Supervisor: Which is not what I said.

Carl: Retrenched.

Supervisor: Right.

Carl: I don't know what that means.

Supervisor: It means there's been a *change* in ... various *needs.* This company needs one thing, and ... you seem to need another.

CARL: I need a job.

SUPERVISOR: Really?

(*Pause.*)

CARL: Yes.

SUPERVISOR (*referring to printout*): That's not what I get from this, Carl. From this I get, uh, "Hey take it easy, I'm not done with my *coffee*," I get, "Where's Carl oh he's in the *bath*room," this kind of thing. And you look at this and say, well this relationship has changed. Obviously. The *needs* have changed. After whatever years. This happens, and no one's to blame. (*Pause.*) Plus this is not the first time.

CARL: Every day I walked in here I was happy to work.

SUPERVISOR: Taken into account.

CARL: I did my best. I never complained. I keep my station clean, I . . . (*Pause.*) All right. What are you gonna do.

SUPERVISOR: Two approaches here, Carl. One, "I'm—retrenched, this is terrible, my life," two, "Change, a good thing, this is what I wanted, maybe I *didn't* know it, but—upward and onward, better times ahead." Which I think is what you're telling me here. Right? (*He taps the printout.*) Big country, Carl. Lots to be done. What are you pulling down here, twenty-three, twenty-four?

CARL: Nineteen.

SUPERVISOR: An *hour?*

CARL: Yah.

SUPERVISOR: Woo, I don't *blame* you. Nineteen no wonder you're fed up. Between you and me, you check out 3M, okay it's a commute, but you know what a junior foreman gets?

CARL: What?

SUPERVISOR: Twenty-two. Twenty-two *base*. Pull down twenty-two you're doing much better. And I *will* give you a recommendation. Forget about this. This is what went on here. We all need a change. You leave, I tear this up. Never happened.

(*Pause.*)

CARL: Well. I'm a free man, I guess.

SUPERVISOR: There you go.

CARL: All you convicts stuck in here.

SUPERVISOR: Hey, don't remind me.

CARL: Maybe I'll take a vacation.

SUPERVISOR: *That's* what you need.

CARL: Cruise on my yacht.

SUPERVISOR: Whatever.

CARL: Round and round. (*Pause.*) You want me for anything else just now?

SUPERVISOR: No. I don't think so.

CARL: Okay.

(*He rises.* SUPERVISOR *starts going through papers on desk.* CARL *stands in the middle of the room, staring at the floor.* SUPERVISOR *looks up. Pause.*)

SUPERVISOR: That's it, Carl.

CARL: Huh?

SUPERVISOR: That's all we need.

(CARL *looks at him.*)

(*Blackout.*)

Scene 2

Later. A bar. CARL, MAN *with a drink.*

MAN (*after a silence*): Mind if I ask you a question?

(*Pause.*)

CARL: No.

MAN: You know the words to the Pledge of Allegiance?

CARL: Yeah.

MAN: Most people don't.

CARL: That a fact.

MAN: It is. They did a study. People don't know what to say in front of their own flag.

CARL: Hmm.

MAN: You read about this lottery winner?

CARL: No.

MAN: Man wins a lottery in Washington State. Twelve million dollars. Been eating dog food to stay alive. Says, "God bless America. This is a dream come true." How do you respond to that?

CARL: He's a lucky guy.

MAN: That's exactly right. He's a *lucky* guy. Comes a point you're either lucky or dead. You a working man?

(*Pause.*)

CARL: Not right now.

MAN: What I figured.

CARL: How's that?

MAN: You look like a fella's got time to think.

(*Pause.*)

CARL: I lost my job today. I don't care. Is that bad?

MAN: Is it?

CARL: Supposed to be.

MAN: *Lot* of things supposed to be.

CARL: I guess.

MAN: Maybe you want to think about *that*.

CARL: Maybe. (*He sips his drink.*) What do they do to this stuff, it's like a chemical.

(*Pause.*)

MAN: My friend, who runs the world?

CARL: *I* don't know.

MAN: Take a guess.

CARL: Ah . . . us. America.

MAN: Nope.

CARL: The Russians. Chinese.

(*The* MAN *shakes his head.*)

Who runs the world?

MAN: I am going to tell you some things you might not want to know.

CARL: Great.

MAN: In October of 1879, Mr. J. P. Morgan sat down at a table with the Jew Baron Rothschild in the city of Vienna, Europe. This is documented. In front of them was a globe of the planet called Earth. They took a cake knife and sawed it straight down the middle. You want to hear some more?

CARL: Sure.

MAN: The Bolshevik Revolution was designed and paid for by the Bank of New York. Fact. Franklin Theodore Roosevelt, he was a great man? In 1934 the International Monetary Fund guaranteed him a crown for prolonging the depression until Japan could mobilize. Here is a surprise. Adolf Hitler, a puppet of the Zionist-Banker Conspiracy, hired to fake the extermination of the Jews. Shot dead in the bunker before he could talk. "What does this got to do with me." This country, the United States we live in, will go bankrupt in 1994, according to a plan drawn up one hundred years ago. Computer simulations in Tel Aviv, Israel for turning New York, Chicago, Los Angeles into death camps. There is literature available on this subject. You understand what's going on now?

CARL: No.

MAN: All this is ending. The world you know. What happened to the farmers, that's just the start. Forces are ruling our lives. We kick ourselves for fucking up the whole time they're rolling us to the furnace in a boxcar. In December of 1987 I was dismissed from my position at Shale Technologies without explanation. Since that time it has been made impossible for me to hold a job. You ever fire a gun into a living human person?

CARL: No.

MAN: Well, you may have to, my friend. If you care about this way of life, you may very well have to. (*Pause.*) Every Thursday at seven-thirty there is a meeting in the Union Hall on Seneca Avenue. I think you need to show up.

CARL: No thanks.

MAN: I'm telling you.

CARL: I'm sorry.

MAN: You will be.

CARL: I have to go.

MAN: In a boxcar, my friend.

CARL: Excuse me, I should have gone straight home. (*He gets up and leaves.*)

MAN (*calling after him*): You keep your eyes open, you're gonna see some things!

(*Blackout.*)

Scene 3

Kitchen table. Night. CARL, *his wife* CATHY. *Sound of jet overhead.*

CATHY: They must have made some kind of mistake.

CARL: They didn't make a mistake.

CATHY: If they had to fire someone—

CARL: I wasn't fired, I was . . . (*Pause.*) Look, when you're in charge you do what you want.

CATHY: It is *not* fair.

CARL: No it's not. And Columbus discovered America.

CATHY: Don't get angry with me.

CARL: I'm not angry at you. I'm not angry at anybody.

CATHY: You should be. After all the promises they made.

CARL: Well.

CATHY: Outrageous.

CARL: They got a big company to run. They can't be worrying about every bug hiding under every rock. That's just understood.

(*Pause.*)

CATHY: I wish you'd come straight home.

CARL: Sorry.

CATHY: I didn't know what happened.

CARL: Okay.

CATHY: I mean they said you left at three o'clock.

CARL: I did. (*Pause.*) Needed a drink.

CATHY: I just wanted to know.

CARL: Now you know.

(*Pause. Another jet flies by overhead.*)

CATHY: Do you . . . think it'll be hard to find another job?

CARL: They always need somebody to do something.

CATHY: What do you suppose you want to do?

CARL: I don't know. We'll see.

CATHY: I could work extra hours.

CARL: You could.

CATHY: At the clinic, you want me to?

CARL: Cath . . .

CATHY: What?

CARL: It's not enough.

(*Pause.*)

CATHY: You can get unemployment.

CARL: Yeah.

CATHY: That'll help.

CARL: I don't want to stand on that line.

CATHY: Maybe you won't have to.

CARL: Two hours on a line begging for pocket change. You know who needs that money? Those food stamp people back of Onondaga Center with the '67 Impalas falling apart all over the yard. And some chewed-up dog taking a dump in the weeds.

CATHY: Don't make fun of them, Carl.

CARL: I'm not making fun of them, honey. That's the last thing I'm doing. (*Pause.*) There's 3M. I can go ask over at 3M.

CATHY: Good idea.

CARL: It's *an* idea.

CATHY: You don't want to be sitting around.

CARL: No, you can't do that.

CATHY: And in the end this is probably all for the best.

CARL: That's right. (*Pause.*) I'll head over there on Monday.

CATHY: What's happening this week?

CARL: Nothing. Nothing is happening this week. I want to take care of some things around the house. As long as I have the time. If that's all right with you.

CATHY: Of course.

CARL: All these things that have to be done. (*Pause. He looks out a window.*) Do we need the porch lights on?

CATHY: Denny's still out.

CARL: Uh-huh.

CATHY: He's going over Spanish with a friend.

(CARL *looks at her.*)

> That's what he told me. I didn't want an argument, I just can't deal with it. I wish you'd talk to him.

CARL: Oh, we talk all the time. We're always yapping away in Spanish.

(*He shuts off the porch light. A jet approaches, very loud.*)

CATHY: Do you want me to rub your back?

CARL: Hah?

CATHY: I'll rub your back.

CARL: I can't hear you.

(*She makes kneading gestures with her hands.* CARL *looks at her blankly. Jet noise. Pause.*)

> (*To himself:*) What is all this?

(*Blackout.*)

Scene 4

The porch. CARL *sitting on the steps, drinking a beer.* DENNY *standing with schoolbooks.*

CARL: Hi.

DENNY: Hi.

CARL: How's everything?

DENNY: Okay.

CARL: Could be better?

DENNY: I don't know. I guess.

CARL: Came in pretty late last night.

DENNY: Wasn't that late.

CARL: Know what you forgot to do?

DENNY: What?

(CARL *looks at him and shakes his head, laughing slightly. Pause.*)

What are you doing here?

CARL: What's it look like I'm doing?

DENNY: Doesn't look like you're doing anything.

CARL: Looks are one thing. What's happening is another.

DENNY: Right.

CARL: You can't not do anything. You're always thinking at the very least. You can't stop doing that. Whether you want to or not. What's your opinion?

(*Pause.*)

DENNY: How come you're home now?

CARL: Because I'm not at work.

DENNY: How come you're not at work?

(*Pause.*)

CARL: Ask your mother.

DENNY: MA, HOW COME DAD'S NOT AT WORK?

(*Pause.*)

CARL: Not everyone appreciates your style of humor, you know. (*He looks at him again and smiles.*) Home from school.

DENNY: Uh-huh.

CARL: How's school, okay?

DENNY: Yeah.

CARL: Getting along with the teachers?

DENNY: I guess so.

CARL: That kid still bothering you?

DENNY: Who?

CARL: The one was bothering you.

DENNY: Uh-uh.

CARL: Well, that's good. (*Pause.*) How's *Spanish?*

DENNY: Huh?

CARL: You doing okay in *Spanish?*

DENNY: Yeah.

CARL: That's one tough language, that Spanish. That takes a lot of extra work. You start in on Spanish, who knows where you wind up. (*Pause.*) We haven't talked in a while.

DENNY: Nope.

(CARL *looks at him. Long pause.* DENNY *stands uncomfortably.*)

Is it okay if I buy a rifle?

CARL: A rifle.

DENNY: A Daisy or a twenty-two or something.

CARL: Why?

DENNY: I don't know. I could learn to use it. Shoot cans and stuff. We could have it around the house.

CARL: Yeah. Yeah, I think you're right. The basement floods, dishwasher breaks down, a rifle really comes in handy. (*Pause.*) Why don't we think about it. (*Pause.*) Mr. Comedian here.

(*Blackout.*)

Scene 5

The living room of a neighbor's house. Evening. CARL, CATHY, TED, JEANETTE.

CATHY (*seated, holding a drink*): Ah *ha* ha ha!

TED (*dancing around the room, wearing an enormous sombrero*): Ai yi yi yi!

CATHY: Oh, it's coming out my *nose* . . .

JEANETTE (*to* CARL): How many times he's done this.

TED: Ai yi yi yi! My pants, they are on fire! Ai yi! Yip yip!

CATHY: Look at him!

CARL: Huh.

TED: Oh muchachos! Ay carumble!

JEANETTE: Ted.

TED: Arriba, arriba!

JEANETTE: *Ted.*

TED: What?

JEANETTE: We *get* the *idea.*

(*Pause.* TED *does a brief flamenco and bows low to Jeanette.*)

TED: Señorita.

(CATHY *giggles.*)

> Who's for a topper? "Me!" Yes sir. (*He pours himself a drink.*) Who else? Cathy?

CATHY (*glancing at* CARL): Why not.

TED: Jenny? Honey? Darling? Beautiful?

JEANETTE: Yes, yes, all right.

TED: Mmmm, I *love* when you say yes.

(CATHY *giggles.*)

> *Someone's* got a dirty mind! Carl! What do you say there, Carl?

CARL: I'll have another, Ted.

TED: *Okay. Okay.* There you go. *Man*-sized. (*He refills Carl's glass.*)

CATHY: Oh, not so much.

CARL: I'm just walking next door.

TED: Everybody ready? Glasses *up.* To, ah . . . to . . .

JEANETTE: Just drink, Ted.

TED: I have my orders. (*He salutes her.*) Up your bottom.

(*They all drink. Pause.*)

CARL: That's a big hat, Ted.

TED: It *is* a big hat, Carl. One the biggest hats I've seen. Got this big hat in the country of Mexico.

CATHY: Oh, you went to Mexico.

JEANETTE: Three hilarious weeks.

CATHY: It must have been wonderful.

JEANETTE: Hmmm.

TED (*with a hayseed accent*): They got these pyramids, same as E-jupt.

JEANETTE: They're not the same.

TED: They ain't? But the man who sold 'em to me—

JEANETTE: Hardy-har.

(*Pause.*)

CATHY: We've thought about Mexico.

TED: Oh, it's the place. *The* place. Cheap as hell. I mean really. Cost us . . . how much it cost us, hon?

JEANETTE: I'm sure I don't remember.

TED: Yes yes yes. Cost us, I don't know, two thousand, tops. First-class, it's too cheap not to go first-class. Now if you want I can—

JEANETTE: Ted.

TED: What?

(JEANETTE *looks at him significantly.*)

What? The *money?* That's not a lot of money. Two thousand dollars is not a lot of money. Carl? Huh?

CARL: No, not a lot.

TED: Uh-*uh.* You got to, excuse me ladies, this is not an insult, you have to ask a man the value of a dollar 'cause *he's* the guy who—

CATHY: I don't know about *that.*

TED: It's my opinion, I'm not ashamed of it.

CATHY: Well.

(*Pause.*)

CARL: You have a language problem down there, Ted?

TED: Actually, Carl, not really. I *speak* a little Spanish—

JEANETTE: You don't speak Spanish.

TED: I said a little, hon, un poco—

JEANETTE: *They* all speak English.

TED: Yeah, you find some English.

CATHY: Well that's good.

TED: Sure, frankly they know where the moola's coming in from, you just got to catch it with a basket—

JEANETTE: You know all about this.

TED: It's part of the *culture*. They are not involved in the work ethic. That, that's an American thing. They're *happy* not to have a job.

JEANETTE: I can't believe you.

TED: What?

JEANETTE: Be a little *sensitive*.

TED: About what?

CATHY: Don't concern yourself.

TED: What, about Carl? Carl, you okay?

CARL: I'm fine, Ted.

TED: Jesus, of *course* he is, he's not a baby. You don't understand him, *I* understand him perfectly. Who are these *women*, Carl? Who *are* they? What are they doing in our *houses*? Carl. Hey, Carl, you know what *you* need?

CARL: What's that, Ted?

(TED *whispers into Carl's ear, then laughs.*)

TED: Right?

CARL: Well.

TED: That'll do you.

JEANETTE: You're disgusting.

TED: I *told* him to take up *gardening.* Give me a kiss.

JEANETTE: Fuck you.

TED (*imitating Woody Woodpecker*): Ah ha ha *ha* ha! (*He kisses her on the cheek. Pause.*) Ooh! Ooh! Guess what *we* got!

JEANETTE: Don't.

TED: It's all ready to go.

JEANETTE: What a waste of money.

TED: I needed it. It's my new toy. Don't go anywhere!

(*He exits. Pause.*)

JEANETTE: Oh, I guess I love him.

(*Silence.*)

CARL: I knew some Mexicans once.

JEANETTE: Did you?

CARL: Yeah. Decent bunch of people.

TED (*offstage*): That's what I'm saying!

CATHY: Where did you know Mexicans?

CARL: Arizona.

CATHY: We weren't in Arizona.

CARL: I was. Before I met you. Eighteen, nineteen years ago.

CATHY: Well.

JEANETTE: What brought you there, Carl?

CARL: Took a summer off. Travel. Find some work. Farm work or something. Get away from home.

CATHY: I certainly never heard about this.

JEANETTE: What kind of farm work?

CARL: Oh, wasn't much of that around.

JEANETTE: So what *did* you do?

CARL: I don't think that I did anything.

JEANETTE: Well. Next time you go, take me along.

CARL: See what I can do.

(*He smiles.* JEANETTE *smiles back.* CATHY *clears her throat. Pause.* TED *enters, holding a video camera with attached floodlight, casting shadows around the room.*)

TED: It's the *Me Show*! With my first guest, Cathy!

CATHY: No, I don't want to be on that . . .

TED: Come on, come on, let's see your stuff.

CATHY: Um . . .

TED: Give us a poem.

CATHY: Oh . . . ah . . . In Xanadu did Kubla Khan a stately pleasure dome decree . . . (*Pause.*) I don't remember the rest . . . please don't make me deal with this . . .

TED (*to* JEANETTE): Honey, you're *on!*

JEANETTE: Stop it.

TED: I'm zooming in, kid, I'm zooming in!

(JEANETTE *strikes a provocative pose and sticks her tongue out.*)

Hubba-hubba!

JEANETTE: Christ.

TED: Your turn, Carl.

CARL: No thanks.

TED: We're rolling!

(*Pause.*)

CARL: What do you want me to do?

CATHY: Do something. Wave your arms.

TED: Try a little Gary Cooper.

JEANETTE: To be or not.

(CARL *doesn't move.*)

TED: Come on, Carl, don't just sit there. This is your chance for fame!

(*He brings the camera in close. CARL sits, squinting in the floodlight, smiling sheepishly. Silence for several seconds. CARL raises his hands like claws and makes a tentative, monster-like growl. Everyone just looks at him. He stands and growls again, louder. He waves his arms.*)

TED: Okay, yeah!

(CARL *lumbers toward* CATHY, *growling.*)

CATHY (*embarrassed, laughing*): Carl . . .

(CARL *grabs her and pulls her toward him. He opens his jaws wide and pretends to sink his teeth into her neck. CATHY screams in mock horror, then laughs hysterically. Still laughing.*)

You're hurting me!

(CARL *buries his face in her neck and keeps growling.*)

(*Blackout.*)

Scene 6

The kitchen. Night, late. CARL *at the table watching a small portable TV.*

VOICE ONE (*on TV*): And I was able to resell that house for fifty thousand—

VOICE TWO: On the *forty*-thousand loan.

VOICE ONE: Uh-huh.

VOICE TWO: That is great. Isn't that great? (*Sound of audience applause.*) Ten *thousand* dollars, Ron, what got you to *try* the no-money-down method?

VOICE ONE: Kip, I—

VOICE TWO: Worked *so* well for you.

VOICE ONE: Kip, I thought I could do better—

VOICE TWO: *Yes.*

VOICE ONE: I wasn't doing badly, but I thought I could do better, my abilities—

VOICE TWO: *How* many months with the no-money-down method, Ron?

VOICE ONE: Four, roughly, months, and I—

VOICE TWO: *Tremendous* results as spelled out step-by-step on the cassettes, Ron, *thank* you for making money.

VOICE ONE: My pleasure, Kip.

VOICE TWO: Wonderful. (*Applause.*) Okay. *What* do we see happening there? We're seeing, yes, The *Formula.* Cash Flow *plus* Discipline *equals* a System. These are the guys you want to get into your life. Cash Flow,

Discipline, System. Ba-da-da, ba-da-da, ba-da-da. Now some people are saying, "Kip, sounds *real* good . . . what does it *mean?* How do I put that on my table?" All right. I want you to listen up close, because we're going to go over exactly what it is you need:

(*Blackout.*)

Scene 7

The kitchen. CARL, CATHY.

CATHY: What do you mean you didn't go?

CARL: I didn't say I didn't go. I said I didn't go *in.*

CATHY: Why not?

CARL: No reason.

CATHY: What . . . did something happen?

CARL: No.

CATHY: To take a drive all the way up there . . . (*Pause.*) Did you drive up there? You didn't, did you? (*Pause.*) Carl?

(*Pause.*)

CARL: They weren't going to hire me anyway.

CATHY: How do you know that?

CARL: Because they're not looking for people like me.

CATHY: That is . . . who are "people like you"?

CARL: I don't know. Who are they. Let's open a magazine, maybe there's a picture of them in there.

(*Pause.*)

CATHY: You need to be doing something, Carl. That's the kind of person you are. You need to have something in your hands, that's what you're good at.

CARL: Yeah, that sounds like me all over. (*Pause.*) I'm gonna wash up for dinner. (*He starts to exit.*)

CATHY: Carl.

CARL: Yah.

CATHY: So where did you go?

CARL: What?

CATHY: You didn't drive up there, where did you go?

CARL: Why?

CATHY: I'm just asking.

CARL: Well, you know, what I did was, I went to the circus, I rented a room downtown and got it on with the bearded lady. Satisfied?

(*Pause.*)

CATHY: I am trying very hard to understand you.

CARL: I don't think I asked you to do that. (*Pause.*) A joke, it's a joke, I'm making a joke. Everything's fine. I love you. I'm looking forward to dinner. I'm really excited about what might be happening for dinner. I been thinking about food all day.

(*Blackout.*)

Scene 8

The kitchen. CARL, DENNY. CARL *fixing a toaster. He takes occasional sips from a pint bottle.*

CARL: Twenty-eight dollars.

DENNY: Uh-huh.

CARL: Explain to me why they cost twenty-eight dollars.

DENNY: I don't know. They just do.

CARL: Sunglasses.

DENNY: They're *special* sunglasses.

CARL: Ah.

DENNY: They have this, um, like filter. That blocks out rays. There are these rays coming in, from space, okay, and more of them are coming in than before. And when the future comes there'll be more than there are now. So everything's gonna get hotter and the North Pole is gonna melt. Nothing will grow and everybody's gonna get cancer.

CARL: From these rays.

DENNY: Yeah.

CARL: And this is worrying you.

DENNY: I'm not worried. It's just what's gonna happen.

CARL: What about your rifle?

DENNY: Huh?

CARL: Thought you wanted a rifle.

DENNY: No.

CARL: Well.

DENNY: Rifle's not gonna do me any good.

CARL: Not like these glasses. (*Pause.*) I'll say one thing I've noticed about you. You're not a conscientious shopper. (*Pause.*) You using that chin-up bar?

DENNY: No.

CARL: Why not?

(DENNY *shrugs.*)

   You use that bar, you might build up your arms.

DENNY: So?

CARL: So you could take care of yourself.

DENNY: So then what?

(CARL *looks away from him. Pause. He reaches into his pocket and takes out a crumpled wad of money.*)

CARL (*giving it to* DENNY): Here.

DENNY: What's this for?

CARL: Your glasses.

DENNY: It's too much.

CARL: No it's not.

DENNY: It is, I can count.

CARL: Take some more.

DENNY: Come on.

CARL (*handing him another wad*): Here.

DENNY: I don't *need* this much.

(*He tries to give it back.* CARL *steps away from him.*)

CARL (*taking out his wallet*): Go ahead. Enjoy yourself. (*He tosses it at* DENNY.)

DENNY: What are you doing, it's too much!

CARL: Hey, you want the car? It's yours.

DENNY: No—

CARL: Don't *lie*, you *want* it. (*He tosses the car keys at* DENNY.)

DENNY: Stop.

CARL: It's free, it's *free*, it's all free!

DENNY: Is this a joke? You're doing something, what am I supposed to . . . (*Pause. He is near tears.*) I don't understand!

(*He stands there with the money in his hands. Pause.*)

CARL: Look at you.

(*Blackout.*)

Scene 9

The kitchen. CARL *in his bathrobe.* CATHY *in overcoat, unpacking groceries.*

CARL: So Jeannie blinks and turns Roger into a billy goat. And that Dr. Bellows guy comes in of course right then and sees, ah, *Tony* standing with a goat. So he shuts the door like "what the hell?" except he accidentally shuts it on his *other* foot, so now it's both legs. And you see Jeannie in Tony's *pocket*, she's you know six inches tall or something, and she's laughing away.

(*Pause.* CATHY *looks at him.*)

See, 'cause she doesn't like Dr. Bellows.

(*Pause.*)

So. That was that. Then I think I watched *Wheel of Fortune*, this woman—

CATHY: It's two-thirty, Carl.

CARL: Uh-huh. Yeah.

CATHY: Are you going to leave the house today?

CARL: I don't think so. I might. I don't know.

(*Pause.*)

CATHY: I can't deal with this, Carl. This is not what is supposed to be. We need money now. Why won't you think about money?

CARL: I have thought about money, hon. I thought about money a lot.

CATHY: And?

CARL: I don't want to do that anymore. I want to think about something else.

CATHY: Like what?

CARL: Well, I can't tell you right now. I'm still trying to work it out. But it's big. It's gonna change a lot of things.

(*Pause.*)

CATHY: Are you involved with someone?

CARL: What do you mean?

CATHY: Are you involved with someone outside this marriage?

CARL: No.

CATHY: Are you telling me the truth?

CARL: Yes. (*Pause.*) Hey, did you remember about the ice cream? I didn't have any breakfast. I keep seeing this beautiful bowl of ice cream in front of me. Like it's floating right . . . there. (*He points to the air before him.*)

(*Blackout.*)

Scene 10

A motel room. JEANETTE *in her underwear, lying on the bed.* CARL *standing, nearly dressed.* JEANETTE *watches him.*

JEANETTE (*after a moment*): Hey, Carl.

CARL: Yah.

JEANETTE: Thanks for inviting me to lunch.

CARL: You're welcome.

(*Pause.*)

JEANETTE: You like secrets?

CARL: They're okay.

JEANETTE: I love secrets. I can't get enough of them. I love knowing them. And I love keeping them. I love keeping them from Ted. Ted's great for keeping secrets from, you know that?

CARL: No.

JEANETTE: He is. You got a secret, keep it from Ted. You'll see how much you like it.

CARL: Old Ted.

JEANETTE: Old Ted. Old Carl. Old me.

(*Pause.*)

CARL: I'm sorry.

JEANETTE: About what?

CARL: I don't think . . . you got what you came here for.

JEANETTE: You don't know what I came here for. Maybe I'm here for the free cable TV. Maybe I'm a spot checker for Quality Inns of America. That's my secret. What's yours?

(*Pause.*)

It's always an awkward situation first out, Carl.

CARL: Oh.

JEANETTE: I enjoyed just lying there with you.

CARL: Yeah. That's lots of fun.

JEANETTE: Are you feeling nervous?

CARL: No.

JEANETTE: Are you feeling guilty?

CARL: No.

JEANETTE: Are you feeling that you have to . . . prove yourself?

CARL: No.

JEANETTE: Then I give up, Carl. What are you feeling?

(*Pause.*)

You know what I always thought about you? What I always found attractive?

CARL: What?

JEANETTE: That you did something very, very terrible. Something that changed your life. And you've never told anyone about it.

CARL: What did I do?

JEANETTE: I think you killed somebody.

(*Pause.*)

CARL: Uh-huh.

JEANETTE: Your best friend or your brother. Or some woman who betrayed you. You were a kid. You shot a man in a holdup, and they never caught you. You were in Vietnam. You had to do things to people, horrible things that no one thinks they can do, but which they find very easy in the end and might even enjoy. You were an alcoholic, a drug addict, you walked around Buffalo or Rochester thinking about needles and picking through garbage. You were a priest, a millionaire, a mental patient. You went to the bottom, Carl, and you saw what there was to see.

(*Pause.*)

CARL: Got me all figured out, huh?

JEANETTE: Do I?

CARL: I hate to disappoint you. But none of that ever happened to me.

JEANETTE: What did?

CARL: Nothing. I'm the guy from across the street. Here I am.

JEANETTE: I like my story better.

CARL: Well, you got to keep yourself happy. That's the big thing.

(*Pause.*)

JEANETTE: Let's start again, Carl. Let's pretend we just walked in. Look at this room. Isn't this a wonderful room? It smells like a new car. Look at this bed. Come lie next to me on the bed. Nobody knows anything about us. Just think of that.

(*She sits on the bed, holding out her arms. Pause.*)

CARL: I got to go. (*He exits.*)

(*Blackout.*)

Scene 11

A room in the Union Hall. CARL, JIM, BOBBY, WALTER (*the* MAN *from the bar*).

JIM: Well, Carl. You're interested in our little group.

CARL: I am, Jim, yes.

JIM: What makes you think this might be the place for you?

CARL: I, ah . . . I can't say for sure, Jim. I ran into . . .

WALTER: Walter.

CARL: Yeah, Walter here, a few weeks back . . .

WALTER: He did that, Jim. He did run into me.

CARL: We got to talking, that is Walter told me some things, I didn't know what to make of them, I . . . and I, I don't know if he told you, I got some time on my hands, sort of between two chairs right now, thought I might come by and . . . try to make some kind of connection. So . . .

WALTER: He's a good guy, Jim, I knew straight away. Really.

(JIM *looks at* WALTER, *then at* CARL. *Pause.*)

CARL: Anyway.

(*Pause.*)

BOBBY: You out of work there, Carl?

CARL: Yah.

BOBBY: How long?

CARL: Six weeks.

BOBBY: Cocksuckers.

JIM: Bobby.

BOBBY: Yeah, Jim.

JIM: *I'm* talking. (*Pause. To* CARL:) Tell me the name of this country.

CARL: United States.

JIM: You know who the king of this country's supposed to be?

CARL: No.

JIM: Every goddamn name in the phone book. Every man who ever lived.

BOBBY: That's right, that's right.

(JIM *looks at* BOBBY. *Pause.*)

JIM: You read the newspapers?

CARL: Yeah.

JIM: Nothing in the newspapers is true. You have to stop reading them.

(CARL *nods.*)

You pay income tax?

(CARL *nods.*)

Then you're an asshole. They got no right to collect income tax. Nowhere do they have that right. That's money you pay them to keep you in jail. You got a kid?

CARL: Yeah.

JIM: Send him to school?

CARL: Uh-huh.

JIM: He doesn't know shit. And that *is* the truth. Now I'm going to ask you a question, and you damn well better answer straight: You look at your wife, look at your *home,* that car you drive, the places you go and *what* they make you do when you show up there and you testify to me: Is that all a *king* is supposed to get?

(*Pause.*)

CARL: No.

JIM: Then why the *fuck* do you take it?

BOBBY: Jim.

JIM (*to* CARL): Huh?

CARL: 'Cause . . . I'm not a king.

JIM: Then *what* are you?

CARL: I couldn't say.

JIM: You can't SAY?

BOBBY: Come on, Jim.

JIM: The fuck are you? Who is this clown? What is he fucking doing here?

WALTER: I invited him, Jim.

JIM: You invited him! Who the fuck are *you? I* don't know him! I don't know what shit he's into! What he wants or, or . . . You know what you give me, *Walter?* Fucking garbage, that's what you bring in here! This, shut *up,* this is an organization! I have *goals,* I have things I am fucking trying to *achieve,* I want to get PUT ON THE MAP. Nothing gets done, absolutely *nothing!*

WALTER: Jim—

JIM: *Fuck* you!

(*He storms out. Pause.*)

BOBBY: IRS is taking him to court. He's under a lot of tension.

CARL: Uh-huh.

WALTER: We don't want you to get the wrong idea.

(*Pause.*)

BOBBY: What we are, Carl, as a group, are patriots. We love this country—

WALTER: I love it.

BOBBY: But something has happened, something is wrong, we're not getting what we need—

WALTER: And we're angry.

BOBBY: We are, angry, and Jim—

WALTER: He's a genius.

BOBBY: We are planning some very big things.

(WALTER *nods. Pause.* JIM *enters.*)

JIM (*calmly*): You got any bucks?

BOBBY: Yeah.

JIM: Let's go to Sharkey's.

BOBBY: Slap some eight ball?

JIM: If you want to lose again.

BOBBY: You wish.

JIM: Six and oh, my man. I'm unbeaten.

BOBBY: Best of ten, Jimbo. You driving, Wally?

WALTER: I promised to be home—

BOBBY: I'll buy you a pitcher.

WALTER: Okay, sure.

(JIM *starts for the door.* BOBBY *and* WALTER *follow.*)

CARL: It's not the income tax.

JIM (*turning back*): You say something?

CARL: It's not the income tax. That's not the problem.

JIM (*coming up to him*): The hell would you know?

CARL: 'Cause I don't see that. I don't feel that.

JIM: You don't.

CARL: No.

(JIM *looks at him. Pause.*)

JIM: Well. I can't believe how lucky we are. Look who walked in? It's Jesus. It's the answer man. Tell me, Jesus. Tell me all about it.

(*Pause.*)

CARL (*to* BOBBY): You feel hungry?

BOBBY: Huh?

CARL: I do. I'm so hungry I can't think of anything else. And all I ever done is waste my time dreaming. Dreaming my *life.* But now I look around I don't know what I was dreaming about. 'Cause it's not here. Now I think we should focus on that. We should work out how to stop all this dreaming so we can see what's really here. That's the first thing we should do.

(*Pause.*)

JIM: That's your "idea," huh?

CARL: Been running through my head. What do you think?

(*Pause.*)

JIM (*to* WALTER *and* BOBBY): Let's roll.

(*They look at him.*)

> Come on.

(*He starts to exit.* WALTER *follows.* BOBBY *doesn't move.*)

> Bobby.

(BOBBY *follows after a moment.*)

BOBBY (*indicating* CARL): What about, ah . . .

JIM (*as he exits, not looking back*): Fuck him, he's nobody.

(*Blackout.*)

Scene 12

The sporting goods section of a department store. CARL *in an overcoat,* SALESMAN *standing before an unseen rack of rifles.*

SALESMAN (*holding a rifle, demonstrating*): Now your average teenager, he's gonna get pretty tired of a pump-action after a couple of weeks. You see the limitations of that gun very quickly. Whereas a twenty-two gives you room to grow. What's he after?

CARL: Not sure.

SALESMAN: Squirrel, raccoon, fox if he's lucky?

CARL: Yeah. Maybe.

SALESMAN: Twenty-two's your man. Light rifle, low recoil, young man's gun. He's what?

CARL: Fifteen.

SALESMAN: Yeah, he could go a long way with this rifle.

(CARL *looks at it.*)

CARL: You sell a lot of these?

SALESMAN: Sell lots of everything.

CARL: What do you sell most of?

SALESMAN: Rifle?

CARL: Yeah.

SALESMAN: Well, this is a good little piece . . . it doesn't suit most people's needs.

CARL: What suits their needs?

SALESMAN: Most people, they're looking for something with a bit more cough to it. Now I want you to look at—

CARL (*pointing at another rifle*): What's that?

SALESMAN: Oh, that's a killer. Throaty monster. That's a nice chunk of gun.

(*Pause.*)

CARL: Let me feel that.

SALESMAN: I'm here to make you happy.

(*Blackout.*)

Scene 13

Later. A bar. CARL, BARTENDER.

CARL: Same again.

BARTENDER: Sorry, pal, we had last call.

CARL (*putting down money*): There you go, let's do it.

BARTENDER: Last call, pal. Time to head home.

CARL: We'll just have another.

BARTENDER: Save some for tomorrow.

CARL: Come on.

BARTENDER: I promise I'll be here.

CARL: Something wrong with my money?

BARTENDER: No. It's a fine-looking bunch of money.

CARL: It is. Now you pour me a drink and I'm gonna give it to you. Nice system, huh?

BARTENDER: Great system.

CARL: I need that and you need this. See, we got something in common.

BARTENDER: Sure we do.

CARL: I bet . . . I bet we watch the same TV programs. You like the *Cosby Show*?

BARTENDER: Yeah.

CARL: Me too. Me too. He's a funny man, a funny man. You eat Big Macs?

BARTENDER: Yeah, I eat them.

CARL: Where do you shop? I bet you shop at the mall, right? I shop at the mall. I bet we put the same kind of gas in our cars. I bet we use the same toothpaste. I bet we think the same way about everything. You know the words to the Pledge Allegiance?

BARTENDER: Uh-huh.

CARL: So do I. We're both Americans.

BARTENDER: You said it.

CARL: And that's gotta count for something. So let's pour me a goddamned drink.

(BARTENDER *looks at him. He starts collecting Carl's glasses.*)

You want my business or not?

BARTENDER: I wanna go home. All good Americans want to go home. You want to go home, don't you?

CARL: I don't see . . . how you get to know . . . what I want to do.

(*He tips the barrel of the rifle out of his overcoat into the bartender's face. Pause.*)

Let me ask you something.

(BARTENDER *nods.*)

Who am I?

BARTENDER: Pal, in my book, you're King of the Hill.

CARL: That's right. That's absolutely right.

BARTENDER: I'm gonna get you that drink.

(*He starts toward the bar.* CARL *jabs the rifle barrel at him.* BARTENDER *flinches. They look at each other. Pause.* CARL *smiles. He walks off.*)

(*Blackout.*)

Scene 14

The kitchen. Before 6 A.M. CARL *sits at the table with the rifle across his lap. Silence.* DENNY *enters from outside, wet and without his shirt. He turns on the kitchen light. He sees* CARL. *Pause.*

DENNY: Hi. (*Pause.*) Did . . . are you waiting up for me?

(CARL *says nothing.*)

See, what happened . . . I was at my friend's house, you know my friend, my buddy Casper, we, okay, the truth I swear, we . . . drank some vodka, his mother said we could, I hardly had any, really, I fell asleep and I just woke up like fifteen minutes ago, I thought, holy shit, excuse me, they don't know where I am. I ran right home. You know Casper. I just woke up. Ask his mother. Swear to God. What a night. Man. (*Pause.*) And she's washing my shirt. (*Pause.*) I better get straight to bed.

(*Pause.*)

CARL: You from here?

DENNY: Huh?

CARL: This country. You speak English pretty good. You got some kind of accent. Most people wouldn't notice it.

DENNY: Look, I swear, you can call his mom.

CARL: You must be from Europe, right? You must be from *Spain*. Well. *Well.* I want to tell you something.

DENNY: What?

CARL: Welcome. Welcome to our shores. And good luck to you. To you and all your people. I mean that, Pedro.

DENNY: Okay.

CARL: Now I'm gonna give you a little advice, something to keep in mind when you're riding up the highways and meeting all the folks and it's this, one thing you should know about this country.

DENNY: What?

CARL: It's three thousand smiles wide. That's right. And I don't know what it's like where you hail from. But around here . . . that's a lot of smiling. (*Pause. He taps the rifle.*) Look what a little money can buy.

DENNY: Did . . . you get that for me?

CARL: Why would I do that?

DENNY: 'Cause I asked you before.

CARL: I don't know what to tell you. You seem like a nice guy. But if you dropped by looking for handouts, you're on the wrong side of the ocean. (*He takes a shell out of his shirt pocket.*) This goes here. (*He opens the breech and loads it.*)

DENNY: I won't do it again, Dad. I promise.

CARL: What?

DENNY: I won't—

CARL: What did you *call* me?

DENNY: *Dad.*

CARL: Pedro, and I can't say this again, but you go around mouthing off in Spanish and you won't make a dime. (*He locks the barrel shut. Pause.*) Comprende?

(CATHY *enters in bathrobe. They look at her. Pause.*)

DENNY: Hi, Ma. Sorry I'm late.

(CARL *snorts with laughter.* CATHY *looks at him.*)

CATHY (*quietly*): You wouldn't waste a second on me, would you? (*Pause. She notices the rifle.*) What are you doing with that?

CARL: I'm sitting with it. I'm enjoying my purchase in the comfort of my home. You got the right to do that here. He'll tell you all about it. (*He gestures toward* DENNY.)

DENNY: See, I was at Casper's—

(CARL *raps sharply on the table with the rifle stock. Pause.*)

CARL: Hey. Who's in the mood for a snack? Who needs a little treat? Pedro?

CATHY: You're stinking drunk.

CARL (*walking over to the cabinets*): Oh you're gonna love this. We got it all here. Anything you could want sitting on these shelves. It's true. (*He opens the cabinets.*) Huh? That's not Spain in there, fella. That's made in the U.S.A. (*He starts taking out cans and boxes, dropping them casually as he names them.*) You want soup? We got it, *Chunky* style! Don't add water. Don't *think* about water! We got Stove Top stuffing. We got Tuna Helper. And it's *good.* Miracle Whip, Cheez Whiz, Creamy Italian *Christ* I'm hungry! You like grape jelly? Sure you do. Who wouldn't like grape jelly? It's America's Favorite. Oh. And look. Look. (*Pause.*) My-T-Fine. You see that pudding? Look how beautiful. You could live in there. That's Paradise. If My-T-Fine won't make you happy . . . I don't know what will. (*He drops the box. Pause.*) Well don't be shy, folks. People are starving in India.

CATHY: Tell me what's wrong, Carl.

CARL: I just got a healthy appetite.

CATHY: Please tell me.

CARL (*handing plates to* DENNY): Let's eat, let's eat!

CATHY: Are you in trouble?

CARL: You know this? "I pledge allegiance—"

CATHY: CARL, I WANT TO HELP YOU. DO YOU UNDERSTAND? TELL ME WHAT YOU NEED.

CARL: One thing I don't need. I don't need people raising their voices.

(*He points the rifle at her. Pause.*)

CATHY (*to* DENNY): Go upstairs.

(DENNY *looks at her.*)

> You heard. Go to your room. Go on. (*To* CARL:) Is that okay?

CARL: No. It's not okay. Actually.

(*Pause.*)

CATHY: What do you think you're going to achieve here?

CARL: I'm not thinking at all. I'm done with that.

CATHY: Then I want you to put that down and come to bed. Tomorrow you're going to get help. You've had a rough time. You were thrown off balance. Inside you're a good man. You have to believe in yourself. Things will get better. You can make them get better. Can't you see that? You have to—

CARL (*pointing*): What's that?

CATHY: What?

CARL: What is it? Right there.

CATHY: Carl—please—

CARL: You tell me what you call it!

CATHY: It's a chair, what do you think it is?

CARL: And what's that?

CATHY: The table, the breakfast table!

CARL: And where are we?

CATHY: Enough, Carl—

CARL: WHERE ARE WE? IT'S A SIMPLE QUESTION.

CATHY: You know where we are. This is our house. This is where we live.

CARL: And who the hell are you?

(*Pause.*)

CATHY: Carl, you put that down. I want you to stop all this right now.

CARL: Okay. (*He pulls the trigger. The rifle goes off.*)

(*Blackout.*)

Scene 15

Another office. CARL, PSYCHIATRIST. *Silence.*

PSYCHIATRIST: Go on.

CARL: Nothing else to say.

PSYCHIATRIST: Can you recall your feelings at the time?

CARL: Oh no. I couldn't do that. I . . . no.

PSYCHIATRIST: Would you say you were angry?

CARL: About what?

PSYCHIATRIST: Man out of work, no gainful employment, he might develop feelings of anger, frustration.

CARL: He might.

PSYCHIATRIST: Could you see that applying to you?

CARL: It's possible. That might take care of your whole problem, right there.

(*Pause.*)

PSYCHIATRIST: Tell me about your wife. Describe her to me.

CARL: A good woman.

PSYCHIATRIST: What does that mean.

CARL: Doesn't mean anything. Good woman. Good person. In over her head a little. Maybe a little. Wasn't her fault. (*Pause.*) And the boy, I always liked him. I don't know why. Funny kid. He could play along with a joke.

(*Pause.*)

PSYCHIATRIST: Mr. Hoberman, are you aware of the conditions of this treatment?

CARL: I believe I am, yes.

PSYCHIATRIST: Would you describe those conditions for me please?

CARL: This or jail.

PSYCHIATRIST: Does the alternative appeal to you?

(CARL *says nothing.*)

Then I must tell you it's in your best interest to be more open with your answers.

CARL: These are the best answers I got. I can't help it if you don't like them.

(*Pause.*)

PSYCHIATRIST: We're going to look at some pictures now.

CARL: Okay.

PSYCHIATRIST: I want you to relax and tell me what you think might be going on in them.

CARL: How would I know that.

PSYCHIATRIST: You can make it up. Whatever you want. There's no right answer. (*He displays a photo of a young girl, sitting on the edge of a bed and looking up.*) Well?

CARL: I couldn't say.

PSYCHIATRIST: Use your imagination.

CARL: I'm no good at that.

PSYCHIATRIST: Then just describe what she's doing.

(*Pause.*)

CARL: She's . . . sitting on a bed. She's looking at something. A picture.

PSYCHIATRIST: Picture of what.

CARL: I don't know. The world.

PSYCHIATRIST: Why is she interested in a picture of the world.

CARL: Well, maybe it's a photograph. Some special kind of photograph. Like they take from out in space.

PSYCHIATRIST: What's special about it?

CARL: Might be a lot in it. A lot of little details. Might show everybody there is walking around all over the Earth. Stuck all over the Earth like tacks or something. And up close you can see 'em, wherever they are, whatever they're doing, business they got, money they're making, it's all in there. Babies waiting to be born, millions of 'em floating around, they're in that picture. And people gone, long time dead, you can see them too, bones everywhere you turn, bones in the dirt, bones knocking together in the ocean, bones sitting inside of mountains. They're all in there. Anyone who is or was or might ever be. But she's not in there. She's not in that picture.

(*Pause.*)

PSYCHIATRIST: And . . . how does that make her feel?

CARL: Don't ask me. I told you I'm no good at this stuff.

(*Pause.* PSYCHIATRIST *looks at his watch.*)

  Time's up.

PSYCHIATRIST: For today I'm afraid.

CARL: No problem.

PSYCHIATRIST (*filling out prescription*): I'm going to start
  you on some medication. Nothing to bother about.
  Get it filled when you have a chance. Two in the
  morning, two before dinner.

CARL: What is it?

PSYCHIATRIST: Antidepressant. It's very effective. Keep
  you on an even keel.

CARL: Why not.

PSYCHIATRIST: If she's up to it, Mr. Hoberman, I'd like to
  bring your wife in. I think that might prove helpful.
  Would you be able to handle that?

CARL: Hmm? Oh, sure. Don't worry about me. You do
  whatever you have to do.

(*Blackout.*)

Scene 16

A coffee shop. CARL, CATHY *wearing sunglasses and a kerchief
tied around her head. Her face looks as if it has recently healed
from a severe bruise. Her left arm is heavily bandaged, partly
hidden by a sweater draped across her shoulders.*

CARL: Order pie or something.

CATHY: No thank you.

CARL: Good pies here. Homemade.

CATHY: I'm sure they're not.

CARL: That's what it says. (*Pause.*) Boy all right?

CATHY: Fine.

CARL: Giving you trouble?

(CATHY *shakes her head slightly.*)

Good, good. (*Pause.*) You're looking a lot better.

CATHY: Am I?

CARL: You're looking like yourself.

CATHY: Well maybe you should shoot me again, Carl. I'll come out looking like a movie star. I'll come out looking like your friend Jeanette.

CARL: Okay, Cath.

CATHY: Only don't drink so much this time. It spoils your aim. (*Pause.*) I don't see what was that bad about our lives, Carl. I don't see what we were missing that a person could reasonably expect to have. I don't understand why you had to smash everything to pieces.

(*Pause.*)

CARL: No reason, Cath. Can't think of one.

CATHY: You son of a bitch. I don't know you at all.

(*Pause.*)

CARL: I got some good news for you.

CATHY: Yes?

CARL: Got a job lined up. Over at 3M. Same stuff, decent pay. Start tomorrow. Night shift but I don't mind the hours.

CATHY: Congratulations.

CARL: So I can send some money over your way. However you want to work it. We can hash it out now, or you can have that lawyer call me. Just tell me what you want.

CATHY: I'll have him get in touch with you.

CARL: Sure.

(*Pause.*)

CATHY: How are you?

CARL: Good, Cath. I'm feeling good. I'm looking on the plus side. I'm keeping on an even keel. Thanks for asking.

(*Pause.*)

CATHY: I have a doctor's appointment.

CARL: Right, you take care of yourself. Nice seeing you, Cath. I'm glad we got to talk. My best to everybody.

(*Blackout.*)

Scene 17

An employees' locker room. CARL, WORKER. CARL *with cup of coffee. They are putting coveralls over their street clothes.*

WORKER: Okay, so here's my problem. I want the three things, the snowmobile, redwood deck for the house, I want that lot in Watsonville 'cause I think it could really take off in a few years.

CARL: Well.

WORKER: See?

CARL: You're in a bind there.

WORKER: I know, 'cause I go over it, and I can't honestly say I need one less than the others. (*Pause.*) Snowmobile would be a kick though.

CARL: That's a nice little toy.

WORKER: But the deck, I need that too. I've needed that for a while. I don't know, you're not interested, are you?

CARL: In what?

WORKER: Halfsies with me on the lot.

CARL: Might be. I'm looking to invest.

WORKER: I should take you over. Good piece of property, preemo location, turn it over like *that*. Way it's going I gotta have something to fall back on.

CARL: Thing is I'm sort of strapped right now.

WORKER: Tell me. I'm squeaking by on this cat chow, it's like a joke. And they're talking pay cuts, right. You were where before?

CARL: Down at ThermoChem.

WORKER: Heard good things about ThermoChem.

CARL: Uh-huh.

WORKER: They start you what, twenty-two, twenty-three?

CARL: Around that.

WORKER: So what made you leave?

CARL: Just between us?

WORKER: You know it.

(*Pause.*)

CARL: Figured I could do better.

WORKER: I hear you, Carl. Loud and clear.

(*He zips up his coveralls.* CARL *takes two pills out of his pocket and swallows them one at a time with his coffee. He sees the* WORKER *watching him.*)

Stomach?

CARL: Keep me from going crazy.

WORKER: Right. Save one for me.

(*A bell rings from the factory floor.*)

Gentlemen, start your engines. And God bless us all.

(CARL *smiles at him. He crumples his coffee cup and throws it in the wastebasket. He stands. He smooths his coveralls.*)

CARL: Time's wasting. Let's make money.

(*He exits, whistling.* WORKER *ties his shoes and follows after a moment.*)

(*Fade-out.*)

THE MIDDLE
KINGDOM

The Middle Kingdom was first presented by the Manhattan Punch Line in New York City on December 3, 1985. The production was directed by Robert S. Johnson, with the following cast:

HUSBAND	Fred Sanders
WIFE	Kathrin King Segal

CHARACTERS

HUSBAND
WIFE
Both in their late thirties

TIME

Night.

PLACE

A kitchen.

Night. HUSBAND *and* WIFE *in bathrobes at the kitchen table, lit by an overhead light.*

HUSBAND: I don't know how to explain this any more clearly.

WIFE: All right.

HUSBAND: It's a matter of numbers, I keep trying to tell you . . .

WIFE: Yes.

HUSBAND: But at this point I don't know what to say except that you've got to start thinking more carefully about money.

(*Pause.*)

WIFE: Would you like some warm milk?

HUSBAND: Do you understand?

WIFE: I'm going to have some milk.

HUSBAND: Hel-looo.

WIFE: Yes, you don't have to speak to me like a child.

HUSBAND: I'm just asking you a question.

(*Pause.*)

WIFE: I understand.

HUSBAND: Well, that's all I wanted to hear. (*Pause.*) What do you understand?

WIFE: I understand . . . I have to be more careful about money.

HUSBAND: Fine. You see? It's that simple.

WIFE: Good.

(*Pause.*)

HUSBAND: I mean I'm just baffled by these purchases.

WIFE: Please, it's late.

HUSBAND: All right, all right, I'm only saying why did you have to buy these things?

WIFE: We needed them.

HUSBAND: *We* needed them?

WIFE: Yes.

HUSBAND: I didn't need this, what's this? (*He holds up a bill.*)

WIFE (*looking at it*): That's the bill to repair your tape deck.

(*Pause.*)

HUSBAND: All right, fine, that's a legitimate expense.

WIFE: It is to you.

HUSBAND: Hold on, this is your tape deck as much as mine. It's part of our home.

WIFE: You yelled at me the last time I used it.

HUSBAND: Because you were using it *wrong*. That's why. If you're going to use it wrong you might as well not use it at all.

(*Pause.*)

Anyway, that's money already spent. It's an investment. You've got to protect your investments, that's just common sense. But *this,* would you mind explaining this to me? (*He holds up another bill.*)

WIFE: That was for a pair of shoes.

HUSBAND: Shoes.

WIFE: Summer shoes.

HUSBAND: I see.

WIFE: What do you mean, "I see"?

HUSBAND: Well, excuse me, but this is exactly what I'm talking about, this is the kind of pointless extravagance that if you'd take a second and *think*—

WIFE: I *needed* shoes.

HUSBAND: Everybody needs shoes, but you don't need "summer shoes," your *feet* don't know what season it is. I mean, why aren't you buying "February shoes" or "low-humidity shoes" or "National Tooth Decay Week shoes," it just seems to me that you're unnaturally involved in this whole shoe thing.

WIFE: You're being ridiculous.

HUSBAND: No, all right, I am, but I'm trying to make a point.

WIFE: I'm not allowed to wear shoes.

HUSBAND: Please, I don't need flippancy, I just want you to start thinking about the bigger picture.

WIFE: Which is.

HUSBAND: Money. The role of money in our lives. My life, and yours, and Aaron's—

WIFE: Aaron is two and a half years old.

HUSBAND: I know that, I know how old my son is, all I'm saying is the things he's learning now will affect him for the rest of his life, and if we teach him properly about money and what it means then he'll be happy.

(*Pause.*)

WIFE: What would you like me to be teaching him?

HUSBAND: Whatever it is he has to know. I'm not here to tell you what to do. But if I were you . . .

WIFE: Yes.

HUSBAND: And I found myself clawing uncontrollably at a pair of "summer shoes"—

WIFE: All *right* . . .

HUSBAND: I'd stop and ask myself, "What bearing will this have on the future?"

(*Pause.*)

Hmm? On the *future*. "What do I want *now*, and what will I *need* later, and which is more important?" That's the basic question any adult has to be able to answer for himself. You see?

(*Pause.*)

Is there any of that babka left?

WIFE: No.

HUSBAND: Damn. I could really go for a slice.

WIFE: I told you to leave some.

HUSBAND: I know, I wasn't thinking. Damn.

(*Pause.*)

WIFE: I'm sorry. Obviously you're much more sensible about this kind of thing than I am.

HUSBAND: Well.

WIFE: No, you're very good about saving and planning and accounts and things like that.

HUSBAND: We all have our talents.

WIFE: It's very manly of you.

HUSBAND: I don't get you.

WIFE: You know, economics. Finances. It's one of those things men like to get wrapped up in. Like your tape deck. One of those male things. Money and machines.

HUSBAND: I don't see why you have to make fun of me.

WIFE: I'm not making fun of you. I'm making an observation. I'm saying it's a subject that men seem to be good at.

HUSBAND: This isn't some kind of test, honey. I'm not trying to prove my virility. I do it for you. I do it because I love you.

(*Pause.*)

WIFE: I'm sorry.

HUSBAND: That's why I do it.

WIFE: I love you too.

HUSBAND: I love you and I *worry* about you.

WIFE: I know you do. Thank you.

HUSBAND: And I can't be there to protect you every second of the day. I'm worried that if you're going around indiscriminately buying shoes and things then there's that much less we have to fall back on. And if the money's not there, if we don't have it where we can't touch it, then we're not as safe as we could be. And I want us to be safe.

WIFE: We're safe enough.

HUSBAND: How can you say that?

WIFE: Because we are. We've got a place to live, we've got clothes on our backs, we're healthy, and we've got a refrigerator full of food. How safe do you want to be?

HUSBAND: The refrigerator's full?

WIFE: I went shopping.

HUSBAND: Good, good.

WIFE: And of course there are things beyond our control—

HUSBAND: Which is *exactly* what I'm *saying*—

WIFE: If a burglar or a crazy man—

HUSBAND: Yeah, so there's a lock on the door, so what? What difference does it make? With all that . . . that . . . *randomness* out there, you've got to secure yourself, you need some kind of protection, right? Something *real*. That's what we've got to think about if we just want to hold on to what we've got *now*. Because otherwise we could be washed away, right off into a ditch with those people you see, you know, they're standing at the bus stop unfolding little bits of paper, and they're asking do you know where some agency or other is they have to go to, because they can't afford to eat, or, or, get some *rash* examined, and you look at their faces and you realize they've fallen clear off the edge of the earth and they don't even *know* it. Because let's be honest, this is America, if you can't make money in this country you're just *stupid*, that's all. You're like a leper and everyone wants to get out of your way. You can walk into a store, you can parade *naked* down the *boulevards* and nobody will even see you because you don't really exist. Because without the money, what are you? Nothing. Invisible. Because the money *makes* you real. That's real, and the rest is bullshit.

(*Pause.*)

WIFE: Is that what's bothering you?

HUSBAND: Me, I'm not talking about me. I'm talking about them.

WIFE: You're just upsetting yourself for no reason.

HUSBAND: I'm not upset, I'm . . . who knows.

(*Pause.*)

WIFE: Would you like me to return the shoes?

HUSBAND: It doesn't matter. No. Yes. No. Do you need the
    shoes?

WIFE: I can live without them.

HUSBAND: Do what you think is best.

(*Pause.*)

WIFE: I really do have to go to bed. I promised I'd get into
    work early.

HUSBAND: Okay.

WIFE: You coming?

HUSBAND: A few minutes.

WIFE: Don't you have to be at unemployment in the morn-
    ing?

HUSBAND: Morning, afternoon, whatever.

WIFE: Well, you shouldn't stay up too late.

HUSBAND: I won't. Good night.

WIFE: Good night. (*Pause.*) People get fired all the time,
    you know. It's not the end of the world.

HUSBAND: Yes.

(*She exits. Silence. He puts her glass in the sink and sits down
again. He shuts off the light. He goes to the refrigerator and
opens it. He stares inside for a while as the lights fade.*)

LIP SERVICE

Lip Service was first presented by the Manhattan Punch Line in New York City on December 3, 1985. Robin Saex was the director. The cast was as follows:

LEN BURDETTE	Peter Riegert
GILBERT HUTCHINSON	John Hallow

CHARACTERS

LEN BURDETTE
a man in his early thirties
GILBERT HUTCHINSON
a man in his sixties

TIME

The present. Over the course of several months.

PLACE

In and around the set of *Sunny Side Up,*
a morning talk show in Roberson City,
an industrial town in the northeastern United States.

Scene 1

The set. GILBERT *and* LEN *seated behind the desk. Pause.*

LEN: Well.

GIL: Hmm?

LEN: History in the making, huh?

GIL: How do you mean?

LEN: Our first show and all.

GIL: Yes, your first. Good luck.

(*Pause.*)

LEN (*doing a bad Bogart*): "Well, Louie, this looks like the start of a beautiful friendship."

GIL: Pardon?

LEN: You know. *Casablanca.* Bogie, end of the movie.

GIL: Ah.

LEN: It's a famous line.

GIL: Afraid I'm not a real student of film.

LEN: Oh. (*Pause.*) Hell, you were probably *there*, right?

GIL: Where?

LEN: Casablanca.

GIL: No.

LEN: Still, you've been around. Korea, right? Vietnam?

GIL: Here and there.

LEN: Don't kid me. I listened to the radio. *"Gilbert Hutchinson Reports!"* Those were something, huh? I remember those. That was journalism.

GIL: That's what we called it. (*Pause.*) Well, those were different times.

LEN: Come on.

GIL: Much different from today.

LEN: Oh sure, well, a lot of the modern conveniences, you didn't have them then. (*Pause.*) Look, Gil, I just want to lay something down here. I mean right off the top of my heart.

GIL: Yes.

LEN: You know I had absolutely nothing to do with this decision.

GIL: I'm aware of that, Leonard.

LEN: I respect you tremendously.

GIL: That's very kind.

LEN: This thing . . . you know what this is? It's a marketing thing. That's all it is, plain and simple.

GIL: Of course.

LEN: And in my book, you're there, you're right there. A-1. You're the peak.

GIL: I'm a hot tamale.

LEN: What?

ANNOUNCER (*voice-over*): Stand by, gentlemen.

LEN: How's my hair?

GIL: Hmm?

LEN: My hair, how is it?

GIL: Fine.

LEN: Feels like I'm wearing a *balloon*.

(*The set lights come up.*)

It's still your show, Gil. I'm just here to help.

GIL: That's nice to know.

ANNOUNCER: Good morning, Roberson City! It's time for *Sunny Side Up*. With your hosts Gilbert Hutchinson and Len Burdette.

(LEN *looks out and smiles broadly.*)

(*Blackout.*)

Scene 2

The greenroom. GIL *and* LEN *are having coffee.* GIL *is looking over some papers.*

LEN: I'll tell you, whatever happens, I am glad to be out of Utah. You've been to Utah, right?

GIL: No.

LEN: Oh my God, *don't* go to *Utah*. Spent eight months there doing *NFL Bleeps and Blunders* on some beanbag indie. Atomic testing, the people there, budabee budabee, you ask for a croissant, they're looking at you like where's your spaceship. Can you get them here?

GIL: What?

LEN: Croissants?

GIL: I think there's a bakery in the mall.

LEN: The mall, that's good to know. This is just much much better. We're talking East Coast, we're talking network *affiliate* . . . much better.

GIL: It's a quiet area.

LEN: Oh, yeah, it's fine, a couple of years, one or two years, establish some credibility, you get some tapes around, you know, over to the network boys . . .

(GIL *looks at him. Pause.*)

Am I bothering you?

GIL (*returning to papers*): No.

LEN: I am.

GIL: I'm just trying to go over the intro copy.

LEN: Really, you do that?

GIL: Habit.

LEN: No, I mean . . . that's great. You *do* that. I'm always meaning to . . .

GIL: It's not that important.

LEN: No, no . . . of course I look at the quiz sheets . . . my style, I like to wing it, you know? Take the guests as they come.

GIL: Hmm.

LEN: Gives a feeling of spontaneity.

GIL: Well, there's that.

(*Pause.*)

LEN: Tradition, huh?

GIL: Pardon?

LEN: That old tradition thing. I hear you. Right right right.

(*Pause.*)

    Gil, I need some feedback, let me bounce this off you.

GIL: Yes?

LEN: A monologue, how would you feel about my doing
    that?

(*Pause.*)

GIL: When?

LEN: Wherever, top of the show, wherever.

GIL: Ah . . .

LEN: You know, a Carson thing. A la Carson. Write it
    myself, topical stuff, nothing heavy. Before we get
    into the guests. A wake-up thing.

(*Pause.*)

    Okay, I dig it. Not in keeping with the show. Say no
    more.

GIL: It's not necessarily—

LEN: It's fine. Really.

GIL: I don't want to reject it outright . . . actually this is
    more Jerry's department . . .

LEN: Well, I met with him, I happened to run into
    Jerry . . .

GIL: Did you.

LEN: Yeah, and he said he could deal with it, but it was
    really up to you.

(*Pause.*)

GIL: Let me think about it.

LEN: Gil, that's all I ask for.

(*Blackout.*)

Scene 3

The set. GIL *and* LEN *at the desk.* LEN *saying goodbye to an unseen guest.*

LEN: Warren, it's been a real eye-opener. I'd say you've given all of us something to dunk in our coffee this morning. Thanks for stopping by. (*He turns out front.*) Okay, once again the book is *Elvis: Child of the Skies* and for anyone who's a fan of the Late Great One— and who isn't—it's pretty special. I'm taking this copy home and reading it under the covers tonight. Gil?

GIL: We'll be speaking with Seventh Ward Representative Adrian Feldenkraus about zoning changes along Hacker Drive when *Sunny Side Up* continues after this.

(*Set lights out.*)

ANNOUNCER: Two minutes, gentlemen.

(*Pause.*)

LEN (*bursting out laughing*): Ah, I love it, I love it, can you believe that guy? With *photographs* no less . . .

(GIL *grunts noncommittally.*)

People, I love people. Geeks, feebs, and clowns, keep 'em coming. I mean . . . (*He starts laughing again.*) Sorry, sorry, I, ah . . . yes, yes, sorry.

(*He controls himself. Pause.*)

The "price of fame," right?

GIL: Hmmm?

LEN: All this Presley crap. Guy's been luncheon meat twelve years.

GIL: Well . . . it's a curious phenomenon.

LEN: Yes, that's exactly, ah . . . it's curious. (*Pause.*) Not that I'd mind it. I wouldn't mind it at all.

GIL: Mind what?

LEN: You know, "fame." The fame thing.

(*Pause.*)

GIL: For what?

LEN: Huh?

GIL: What would you be famous for?

LEN: Ah . . . for . . . being me. I mean . . . what do you mean? I don't know what you mean.

(*Blackout.*)

Scene 4

Backstage of studio. LEN *on the phone with his wife.*

LEN: No, I guess I *don't* see the problem, you know I like a croissant in the morning, what's the big . . . At the mall . . . the *mall*, the fucking mall . . . No, I don't, but this is an American city, the people speak English, you get in the car and . . . What? What? Who told you that? . . . No I did not . . . No I did not . . . No I did . . . What time I came home, who cares? . . . Listen, your sister is a guest, tell her to keep her nose . . . No, fuck her, I don't give two shits in hell what your sister . . .

(GIL *enters.*)

LEN: Yeah, you heard me. Fuck your sister, fuck your brother, fuck your fucking father, and fuck you.

(*He hangs up. He sees* GIL.)

    My wife.

GIL: Ah.

LEN: We're having a little disagreement.

GIL: Oh.

ANNOUNCER: Places, gentlemen.

(*Blackout.*)

Scene 5

GIL *behind a podium. Pasted on the front, a sign:* "CAREER DAY." *He addresses a high-school assembly.*

GIL: My job . . . is to watch. I watch things go by. That's what I'm paid for. To watch, and to comment. Now I can see that some of you are smiling, perhaps you're thinking that's not such a very hard thing to do. Not as hard as being a bricklayer, for instance. Or driving a bus.

(*Pause.*)

    Well, maybe you're right.

(*Pause.*)

    I've been watching things go by for nearly forty years now. That's more than twice as long as you young men and women have been alive. Except perhaps for those of you who have been left back.

(*Pause.*)

Do they still leave people back? Or has that gone the way of the inkwell? No?

(*Pause.*)

And in that time the world has undergone the most sweeping changes. Changes of a positive nature. I've been fortunate to have been a witness to many of them. For example . . . ah . . .

(*Pause. He has lost his place.*)

Ah . . . the men on the moon . . . and the, ah . . .

(*Pause.*)

As I look out over your faces I wonder what kind of world we have bequeathed to you. What hopes you can have. What can possibly . . . just what can be done now.

(*Pause.*)

And . . . so . . . the topic at hand. Broadcasting as a career. Opportunities. The opportunities are greater than ever. As information increases, the need for qualified people to disseminate that information also . . . increases. Rapidly. All you need is the desire to communicate. To those of you who have that desire . . . good luck. And, of course, stick with it.

(*Pause.*)

If there are any questions I'll be glad to . . . yes, the young lady with the, ah, hair.

(*Pause.*)

Yes, I'm afraid he is married.

(*Blackout.*)

Scene 6

The control booth. LEN *and* GIL *are watching a playback on the monitor.*

LEN: Now this is it, look what he does right here. You see that? He cuts to a two shot. *I'm* asking the question, *I'm* the one people should be looking at. I say come in tight, give me a tight shot there and stop fucking around, nobody wants to see that no-name twat with her tits hanging out which you can't see *anyway* so why is she there in the first place, what, you're looking at me, do I have food . . . Oh boy. I'm sorry. Get the soap.

GIL: Excuse me?

LEN: You must think I really hate women, right?

GIL: Why would I think that?

LEN: What I just said about her, you know . . .

GIL: Well, you seem to be upset. Just blowing off steam.

(*Pause.*)

LEN: I am?

GIL: I thought so.

LEN: Wow. You are great, Gil. You really are.

(GIL *smiles.*)

> No, I mean it. I didn't even *know* that. And you take one look at me, zap, "you're blowing off steam." That's what makes you a journalist. I've got a lot to learn from you.

GIL: It was simply an observation.

Len: Yeah, well *I* wouldn't have observed it. That's all I can say.

Gil: I like to think I'm a pretty decent judge of character. My one gift.

Len: Mr. Modesty here. Man's broken bread with half the names in the encyclopedia. You interviewed Nixon in the fifties, didn't you? I bet you had him pegged in a second.

Gil: No.

Len: Come on.

Gil: I didn't interview him.

Len: You didn't? Are you sure?

Gil: I never reported from Washington.

Len: Hmm. I could have sworn it was you. (*Pause.*) Gil, let me plug into you for a sec.

Gil: Plug away.

Len: Am I coming on too strong?

Gil: In what way?

Len: On camera. Am I coming on too strong on camera?

(*Pause.*)

I am, aren't I?

Gil: I didn't say that.

Len: Tell me if I am. I need to know.

(*Pause.*)

Gil: It's hard for me to judge. We're both up there . . . you can't really tell how it comes across. The camera . . .

Len: Camera's a bitch. She's just a real bitch.

GIL: They seem to like you out there.

LEN: They do?

GIL: That's the impression I get. The new format . . . it seems to be a good mix.

LEN: Oh, the mix, the mix is great.

(*Pause.*)

Gil, I just want to tell you, these last few weeks have been a real pleasure for me.

GIL: Well, Leonard, I've enjoyed having you aboard.

LEN: You have.

GIL: A little change never hurt anybody.

LEN: No, you're right, you're so right. Thank you, Gil. That means a lot to me.

(*Blackout.*)

Scene 7

Night. GIL *at home in front of the television.*

ANNOUNCER'S VOICE (*on TV*): Tomorrow morning, make sure you start your day right. Start it with a *Sunny Side Up*! WICZ's good-morning talk show gets you going with a smile where it counts. Hosts Len Burdette and Gilbert Hutchinson will tickle your funny bone while they open your eyes with the news of the world!

LEN'S VOICE: No, but I love the President. If *he's* relaxed enough to take a nap, what do we have to worry about?

(*Audience laughter.*)

WOMAN'S VOICE: And this is Max. He's just a baby. When he grows up he'll be over twenty feet long.

LEN'S VOICE: He's real cute, could you keep him out of my trousers?

(*Laughter.*)

GIL'S VOICE: Talks are expected to continue until the Thursday night deadline . . .

LEN'S VOICE: I'm not sure if you're supposed to eat this stuff or wear it!

(*Laughter.*)

ANNOUNCER'S VOICE: So treat yourself right, Roberson City! Wake up to the *good* morning vibes of *Sunny Side Up*. Weekdays at nine. Here on ICZ—we're your family!

SIGN-OFF VOICE: At this time, WICZ concludes its broadcast day. Join us tomorrow morning at six for *Jump Up With Dave*. Good night.

(*Blackout.*)

Scene 8

The makeup room. GIL *and* LEN *in the chairs.*

LEN: Well, I hope *you're* feeling good today.

GIL: Nothing to complain about. Looking forward to the show.

LEN: Good. Good for you. At least somebody's happy.

(*He sighs heavily. Pause.*)

GIL: You seem a little preoccupied.

LEN: Oh boy. I knew I couldn't hide it from you, Gil. No point trying.

(*Pause.*)

GIL: Well, whatever it is, I'm sure it'll work out for the best.

LEN: I don't *know*, Gil, I just don't.

GIL: Well.

(*Pause.*)

LEN: Gil, do you find me attractive?

GIL: In what way?

LEN: I mean, I respect your opinions, you know that. Would you say there's something about me that's naturally attractive?

GIL: To women?

LEN: Basically.

GIL: Well . . . I'd say you're a . . . pleasant-looking man.

LEN: Hmm.

GIL: Women would probably notice that . . .

LEN: Yeah, yeah.

GIL: I'm sure it's something you're aware of.

LEN: Gil, I know this sounds terrible, but I cannot help it. It just comes across, no matter what I do. Isn't that ridiculous?

GIL: Yes.

LEN: I genuinely like people. They can see that. They respond to it. It's nothing mysterious.

GIL: I suppose not.

LEN: But try telling that to my wife.

GIL: Ah.

LEN: You know what I'm talking about. We're out there, you and me, we're coming into people's *homes,* we're establishing a bond. We're offering friendship. *Through* the *medium.* And when the audience wants to return that friendship . . . well, that's the greatest reward a personality can hope for, isn't it? But what I say to her, I say, "What you see and what actually *happens* . . . are entirely different things." Huh? No matter what it might look like.

(*Pause.*)

You're married, right?

GIL: Divorced.

LEN: Ho ho, tell me about it. This is number three for me. Juggling that old personal life, eh? That career/personal life thing. El bitcho.

(*Pause.*)

Messy?

GIL: What?

LEN: Yours, messy?

GIL: Yes. Yes, it was.

LEN (*showing the back of his hand*): See that? Right there? Number two. A cocktail fork, straight through to the palm. Looked like a horror movie. I don't even want to think what this one would do. But like the man says, you can't make an omelette.

GIL: No, I guess you can't.

(*Blackout.*)

Scene 9

The set. GIL *and* LEN.

GIL (*out front, to unseen camera*): . . . The position of both nations continues to be untenable. Nuclear disarmament should not be an excuse for ruffling the feathers of patriotic pride nor a playground for the paranoid delusions of militaristic minds. As the hands of the clock approach dead midnight, it is past time for the cry of the last sane voice to be heard. That voice is ruffling the feathers of patriotic . . .

(*Pause.*)

That voice is crying for peace. This has been Gilbert Hutchinson with today's view on the news.

LEN: And we're making bye-byes because *our* time is up here on Sun*ny* *Side* *Up.* Be here tomorrow aloha 'cause we'll be talking with Roberson City's own lovely Marguerite Linx, you've seen lots of her on *Superstar Hardbodies,* I know we'll all be rising to the occasion there. Right, Gil?

GIL: Ah . . .

LEN: Okay! While Gil recovers from electroshock, this is Mrs. B's boy saying sayonara from . . . *Sunny Side Up!* We love ya!

(*Set lights out.* GIL *rises.*)

LEN: Whoa, Gil, hold on there, I didn't mean that.

GIL: Hmm?

LEN: The electroshock gag. I'm sorry.

GIL: Did you say that? I wasn't listening.

LEN: I caught you there and it was the first thing that popped into my head. I was only trying to cover. I didn't *mean* anything by it.

GIL: You were making a joke.

LEN: Yes, exactly. Just to cover the hole.

GIL: I'm not totally humorless, you know.

LEN: No, I never—

GIL: I know a joke when I see one.

LEN: As long as you understand. (*Pause.*) Can't have dead air, right? Rule number one.

GIL: I lost my place.

LEN: Listen, that can throw you.

GIL: Yes.

(*Pause.*)

Afraid I've got to run.

LEN: Oh, sure. Sorry.

(*Pause.*)

Gil.

GIL: Yes?

LEN: You okay?

GIL: You bet.

(*Blackout.*)

Scene 10

LEN *in front of a mirror, practicing.*

LEN: Hello, everybody! . . . Hel*lo*, everybody! . . . *He*l*lo*, everybody! . . . *Hello everybody!* . . . Hello . . .

(*Blackout.*)

Scene 11

The cafeteria. LEN *and* GIL *with food trays.*

LEN: You've got to hear this gimmick. Hear the gimmick, then you can eat. This is the gimmick. We get one of the minis from the newsboys, we set up downtown— no, no, we stick it in the *mall*, I go around, I pick out the weirdest-looking people I can find, and I ask them . . . to imitate their favorite animal.

(*Pause.*)

GIL: And?

LEN: And then we show it.

GIL: Why?

LEN: To show how *weird* people are.

(*Pause.*)

And also . . . how important it is to laugh at yourself.

GIL: I don't think we have the time.

LEN: Time, we can make the time.

(*Pause.*)

GIL: You'll have to talk to Jerry about it.

LEN: Well, Jerry and I, we did the basic groundwork on this.

GIL: You're saying this is Jerry's idea?

LEN: I'm not saying it's anybody's *idea*. I'm just saying he went over the groundwork with me.

GIL: I see. (*Pause.*) Well, I think it's wonderful.

LEN: You do?

GIL: Oh yes. Inspired. That's the word I'd have to use. I love what it's trying to say and it adds so much to the show. I think we should have more features just like it, as many as possible, all the time.

LEN: Well, I'm glad you—

(GIL *turns and abruptly exits.*)

Hey, Gil, what's going—Gil! . . . Gil, are you coming back? You left your tray! (*To a person on line in front of him:*) He's coming right back.

(*Blackout.*)

Scene 12

LEN *in a bar, talking to a woman.*

LEN: What's it like? It's no big deal. I mean, you're just talking to people. That's all it is, just talk. I like it because I'm really *into* people, listening to them. You know, conversation. Like we're having now. We're

talking, right? We're *communicating*. And that's all
that really matters. Whether I'm sitting next to you
or Joan Collins, or what the hell, Michael *Jackson* or
somebody . . . Hmm? I sure have. And believe me it is
not an act, that man is as sweet as a baby. Now the way
I see it, it's a new world, new game, new rules, huh?
You know that most of the people who were ever born
are alive right now? It's true. Isn't that so interesting?
There's no *time* anymore for "Hi, hello, nice to meet
you," or getting to *know* you, that stuff. I am a gut
person, I'm very connected to my gut, and when —
What? . . . Am I married? Am I married? Come on. I
thought we were communicating here . . . No, it's
fine. (*Pause.*) Hey, you want to do a fun thing? Let's do
a fun thing. I want you . . . to imitate your favorite
animal.

(*Blackout.*)

Scene 13

The parking lot. GIL *and* LEN *in overcoats.*

LEN: I hate this. I would give my bank account to be in
California right now. My nuts feel like they're in an
ice cube tray. Is this your car?

GIL: Wha . . . no.

(*Pause.*)

LEN: Look, the important thing, don't make it worse than
it is.

GIL: No.

LEN: Jerry's just doing what he's told. Those guys upstairs, they get little printouts on their desks, they

make a decision, they don't know what's going on out
here. All they see are numbers. Anyway . . .

GIL: Anyway it's out of my hands.

LEN: Basically, yes. This your car?

GIL: No.

(*Pause.*)

LEN: And what difference does it make where you *sit*,
huh? So you're sitting on the couch now. So what.
Whoop-dee-do.

GIL: Yes. Of course.

LEN: You sit behind the desk, you sit on the couch, it's all
the same. The same show.

GIL: Just the same.

LEN: Look at Ed McMahon. *He* sits on the couch. You
think he minds? Guy's got more money than Canada.

GIL: Yes.

LEN: Fucking *billions* of dollars.

GIL: I'm sure he's very comfortable.

LEN: And as far as I go, this is still half and half. I want
you up there, I want you with those tough questions—

GIL: They took away my commentary.

LEN: Yeah, well, they did that. *But* let's try and see it from
their side. I mean, the commentary was fine, it was
just beautiful, but it was really kind of a little out of
place. For a wake-up show. People just aren't *into* the
commentary thing in the morning. And on the other
hand we've got some time to play around with now.

GIL: Time for what?

LEN: I don't know, for whatever it is we've got the time for, is this your car?

GIL: I've been doing it for ten years.

LEN: Okay, but that was that, this is this. If they want commentary, let 'em read the Bible.

(*Pause.*)

Which is a great book, don't get me wrong.

(*Pause.*)

I mean . . . I don't know what I mean, I'm freezing my ass off. Sweet Jesus, please let me be some place else next winter. I gotta go.

GIL: Am I keeping you?

LEN: No, you're not. Good night.

GIL: Yes.

(LEN *starts walking away.*)

Leonard.

LEN: Yeah, Gil.

(*Pause.*)

GIL: Could I impose upon you for a ride? I can't remember where I'm parked.

(*Blackout.*)

Scene 14

The set. LEN *interviewing a guest.* GIL *sitting on the couch, looking out front.*

LEN: Ah ha.

(*Pause.*)

Yah.

(*Pause.*)

Ah ha.

(*Pause.*)

Really? That's fascinating.

(*Pause.*)

That's *really* fascinating.

(*Pause.*)

Ah ha.

(*Pause.*)

Well, you look it!

(*Pause.*)

No, no, I mean that as a compliment.

(*Pause.*)

Who do you play with?

(*Pause.*)

Oh, he's one of my favorite people. He really is.

(*Pause.*)

Ah ha.

(*Pause.*)

Now isn't that interesting. I never realized that.

(*Pause.*)

Well, that's interesting.

(*Pause.*)

Now that's *really* interesting.

(*Blackout.*)

Scene 15

The greenroom. GIL *and* LEN. GIL *smoking a cigarette. Silence.* LEN *looks at* GIL. *Pause. He looks away. Pause. He looks at him again. He is about to speak.*

ANNOUNCER: Places, gentlemen.

(*Blackout.*)

Scene 16

GIL *at home, on the phone.*

GIL: Hutchinson . . . Yes, Jerry, hello . . . I'm fine . . . Yes, I'm relaxing . . . Do you have something . . . Can we leave it for Monday? . . . All right.

(*Long pause.*)

I see.

(*Blackout.*)

Scene 17

LEN *on the set.*

ANNOUNCER: *Sunny Side Up* with Len Burdette!

LEN: Hello, everybody! Hope you're feeling bright tailed and bushy eyed this morning. Well, looks like I'm all on my lonesome here at the majestic ICZ broadcast palace 'cause Galloping Gil Hutchinson has took himself off for the kooky Caribbean, I kid you not, leaving me high and dry, well, dry at least for who knows how long. Gil, if you're watching, and who wouldn't be, knock back a few piña coladas for moi!

(*Blackout.*)

Scene *18*

A bar. GIL *sits with a drink.*

LEN (*entering, speaking off*): No, you sit, I'll get it! (*He sees* GIL.) Oops.

(GIL *looks up.*)

Hey, hey, look at this, look at this!

GIL: Leonard . . .

LEN: Just *look* at this! Look at you, you look great! Look at this!

GIL: How are you?

LEN: How am I? How am *I*? Look at this! I didn't know you came here, what are you doing here?

GIL: Drinking.

LEN: Drinking, of course you're drinking, you're in a bar. Look at you, how the hell *are* you, is that a tan there?

GIL: Where?

LEN: On you, where. Dry, very dry. So hey, how was it?

GIL: How was what?

LEN: Look at this, I'm playing straight man. Your trip.

GIL: I haven't been on a trip.

LEN: No, not now, *before.*

GIL: I haven't gone anywhere. I've been here.

LEN: So . . . you've been home, huh, taking it easy? That's good. Travel, what a pain in the ass, give me a few days at home, plenty of beer, turn on the TV—well, not the TV, I didn't mean—that's good, so you've been home, you've been doing, what . . .?

GIL: I've been doing nothing.

LEN: Doing nothing, okay, okay . . . hey, guess what?

GIL: What.

LEN: Check out the beehive blonde there. Over there by the ferns?

GIL: Yes.

LEN: Say hello to number four.

GIL: Well.

LEN: She nabbed me, man. I got glued, bam. Meantime the other one's sucking it out of me with a straw. I'm thinking about a bodyguard, seriously. Guess where I met her. The mall.

GIL (*at the same time*): The mall.

LEN: Yeah, did I already say that?

GIL: You must have mentioned it.

(*Pause.*)

LEN: Well, Gil.

GIL: Yes.

LEN: Gil Gil Gil. My heart was breaking. You know that.

GIL: I didn't.

LEN: The way things worked out? It just broke my heart. What can I say?

GIL: Very kind of you.

LEN: God knows what they had in mind. I told them they were making a mistake, but who the hell am I, right?

GIL: On the button.

LEN: They are killing it, Gil. They're killing the medium. They can't *appreciate*—I mean, you and me, we were together. We were a team, like—

GIL: Abbott and Costello.

LEN: Yeah, them, or Huntley and Brinkley, and that kind of relationship needs *time* . . . ah, what are you gonna do. It's a shitty business. You were smart to get out when you did. I'm sick of it.

GIL: Are you?

LEN: I'm sick of *this*. I want out of here. This whole thing with Jerry—you know about the thing with Jerry?

GIL: No.

LEN: Well, I can't get into it. But he's limited, he's very limited. Fortunately, and I shouldn't even be saying this, but—cable. A cable deal. Nothing definite. But it looks good. And you know, I can't make any promises, but I'm gonna need people, good people around me—

GIL: Maybe I can do the weather.

LEN: That's an idea.

GIL: Maybe I can do it as my favorite animal.

LEN: Well, or something . . .

GIL: I'm not interested.

(*Pause.*)

LEN: No, you know what you should do, Gil? This just popped into my head, but you should write a book. I mean with all the biggies you've sat down next to, you could write one hell of a book. I know I'd read it. I'd love a book like that. Have you thought of that, of a book?

GIL: No.

LEN: You should.

GIL: I don't know any "biggies."

LEN: Come on.

GIL: I don't.

LEN: Sure you do.

GIL: I don't. Why do you insist on saying that? Can't you listen to what I tell you? Is it that difficult? I am not famous. I do not want to be famous. I do not know famous people. I had a job. I sat behind a desk and read copy into a microphone. Then I read copy into a television camera. I am no longer doing that. I am very tired and I want to sit here and drink a lot of Scotch. Do you understand?

LEN: I understand you're a little upset . . .

GIL: You think I'm *upset.*

LEN: Well, I think you're . . . blowing off some steam . . .

GIL: Dear God.

LEN: Now, I know you pretty well—

GIL: No you don't. You don't know me at all. I don't want you to be my "friend." I don't want you to know anything about me.

LEN: All right, all right—

GIL: You can't even talk to people without humiliating them!

LEN: Gosh, Gil, I'm only making conversation.

(*Pause.*)

GIL: It's strange. You look like a human being, you speak clearly enough, and yet I have absolutely no idea what it is you're trying to say. Why do you suppose that is?

LEN: Hmm, well, I don't know, Gil. That's an interesting question. It really is. I'm gonna think about that. Hmm.

(*Pause.*)

I gotta get moving, Gil. Great talking to you. (*He exits.*)

(*Blackout.*)

Scene 19

The set. LEN *behind the desk.*

LEN: And we are back here at *Sunny Side Up,* the show that dares to ask the question "What's the most disgusting thing you've ever stepped in," let's avoid the obvious answers please, we'll be taking your calls in just a while, remember the winner will be receiving free bus fare to downtown *and back,* yes, and a complimentary pocket comb from the entire janitorial staff here at ICZ, I know *I* couldn't resist it, I see our happy-go-lucky director Jerry signaling me, and let me just show you what Jerry has given me here, can the camera pick this up? It's a mechanical chimp, folks, just like the astronauts use, and it says right here on the back, "Happy three years on ICZ." Yes folks, three warm, wonderful, and why not come right out and say it, just plain wacky years. Jerry, thank you, I know where you live.

(*Pause.*)

And time munches on, indeed it do, and, ah . . . boy it's cold out, huh? Isn't it cold? You folks at home just nod. We're having some fun now.

(*Pause.*)

Okay, our neck guess . . . blah, I mean our *next guest,* very good, Len, is a familiar face to a lot of folks here, he's, ah, a distinguished newscaster, and he's written a book, and I hear it's selling pretty well, and his name is . . . Gil Hutchinson. Come on out here, Gil.

(GIL *enters.*)

LEN: Gil, it's great to see you.

GIL: Len, I'm happy to be here. Hi, Jerry!

LEN: Now, Gil—

GIL: Dead trout, front seat of my car. Squish!

LEN: What?

GIL: I stepped in it, I kid you not!

LEN: Ha, yeah, that *is* disgusting.

GIL: You wanted to know.

LEN: Well, ah . . . (*holding up book*) *My Side of the Micro-phone*. Great title—

GIL: *Thank* you.

LEN: How'd you *think* of that?

GIL: Sort of popped into my noggin, seemed to fit.

LEN: That's great, and it's sort of—

GIL: What it is, Len, is a memoir about the early days of broadcasting. Those seat-of-your-pants, get-your-hands-dirty days. Great stories, *great* times.

LEN: Sort of a what, an, an, *analysis* of the changes—

GIL: Whoa, "analysis" he says! Len, it's more of a people book. It's a book *about* people *for* people.

LEN: Broadcasting.

GIL: Those great early days.

LEN: Nothing about the later days in there, huh?

GIL: Oh no. That's a whole nother story.

(*Pause.*)

LEN: Gil, book, success, surprised?

GIL: Len, I've got to tell you, there's nothing like it. It feels *great*.

LEN: Well, you deserve it after all these years.

GIL: Hey, better than never, huh?

LEN: Right . . .

GIL: You know how *that* feels!

LEN: Well, I . . . Yeah. Great. Really interesting. Ah . . . I'm going to read this, I am. Can I have this copy?

GIL: I'd rather you bought one.

LEN: Ha, I *love* it! (*Pause.*) Gil, you are looking *great.*

GIL: Len, I *feel* great.

LEN: Well, you *look* great.

GIL: It's great to *be* here.

LEN: It's . . . great . . . *talking* to you.

GIL: It *is* great to talk, Len. Really is. Sitting here . . . talking to you, like this . . . it's just the greatest thing there is.

(*Pause. They look at each other.* LEN *can't think of anything to say.* GIL *smiles broadly.*)

(*Blackout.*)